LIONS IN THE...

LIONS AND FALCONS

LIONS AND FALCONS
My Diary of a Remarkable Year

Jonny Wilkinson
with Neil Squires

HEADLINE

First published in 2001
by HEADLINE BOOK PUBLISHING

10 9 8 7 6 5 4 3 2 1

British Library Cataloguing in Publication Data

Wilkinson, Jonny
Lions and Falcons: my diary of a remarkable year
1. Wilkinson, Jonny 2. Rugby football players – Great Britain –
Biography
I. Title
796.3'33'092

ISBN 0 7472 4238 0

Typeset by Avon Dataset Ltd, Bidford-on-Avon, Warks

Printed and bound in Great Britain by
Mackays of Chatham plc, Chatham, Kent

HEADLINE BOOK PUBLISHING
A division of Hodder Headline
338 Euston Road
London NW1 3BH

www.headline.co.uk
www.hodderheadline.com

Contents

Acknowledgements

In putting together this book my thanks go to my mum and dad for their help and support and to my brother Mark for his alternative viewpoint and memory when mine failed me. Thanks also to Tim Buttimore and Simon Cohen for their organisation and assistance and to my ghost, Neil Squires, for his patience and skill. Finally to all the players and coaches involved with Newcastle, England and the Lions – thank you, too. Without you all I would have nothing to write about.

chapter one

Under the knife

The nurse wielded the razor like an expert. She had obviously done this sort of thing before. She was an attractive girl whose routine job at the Princess Grace Hospital in London that sunny July morning was to shave a rugby player in preparation for a groin operation. Looking down the bed at the top of her head and trying to carry on an ordinary conversation while she tinkered around in my pyjamas was not easy. I mean, what do you talk about? The weather? I muttered a few inadequate platitudes.

For the nurse, it was just another day at the office. For the patient, it was a lot more than that. It was the beginning of a process that would decide whether my dream of becoming a British Lion could come true. Ahead lay the longest season in professional rugby history – August 2000 to July 2001 – a choppy passage through players' strikes and foot and mouth to Cup finals and the Six Nations Championship, culminating in the Lions tour to Australia. But if this didn't work . . .

I was nervous. Apart from a minor scrape that involved removing an abscess from my calf as a teenager, I had never undergone an operation before. They are part and parcel of professional sportsmen's lives, particularly rugby players because of the physical nature of the game, but this was brand new to me.

The pain in the right-hand side of my groin had sprung up during the latter part of the 1999–2000 season. I hadn't been able to train properly between matches and what I did in games had been a little restricted. Newcastle and England helped me keep quiet about and deal with the difficulties I was having and we all played it down when news of the injury eventually leaked out. It was a lot worse than anybody on the outside knew.

I was aware something needed to be done but it still came as quite a shock when I was told I needed to go for an operation. I was advised to miss England's summer tour to South Africa. I sought out a second opinion from Jerry Gilmore, a specialist who had performed the same operation successfully on Martin Johnson. He said he thought I could go on tour if I managed the problem sensibly but recommended coming straight into theatre on my return. So I flew back from South Africa on my own the day after we had beaten the Springboks in the second Test in Bloemfontein, leaving the celebrations behind.

I quite enjoy flights usually. Playing for England means travelling business class which involves a lot of pampering and you can't beat a bit of that. When a stewardess isn't offering this, that or the other, I'm often sound asleep. I'm a world-class snoozer on any form of transport. However, on the flight back from South Africa I just could not sleep. It may have had something to do with being beaten up by the Boks at altitude – I felt like I was in a permanent bearhug – but thoughts of the operation ahead were also affecting me. Preparing for the international had filled all my waking hours but with that out of the way I was suddenly confronted by the stark reality of what lay ahead.

I had talked to a few other players about the operation, most of whom were supportive – not everyone, though. Some were quite sceptical. Groin problems seemed to be endemic for rugby players and some had threatened to end careers. Jerry Guscott and Dan Luger had both been out for over a year.

As I lay in the hospital bed, I was confident my operation would be a success but, trying to peep into the theatre from my adjoining room, I couldn't help but feel vulnerable. There I was, in a back-to-front gown, waiting to have my insides rearranged.

I turned to the television for comfort and found myself watching tennis from Wimbledon. With the sun streaming in through the window, I couldn't have asked for anything more therapeutic. Whenever I see those famous grass courts I come over nostalgic. The dull thud of racket on ball, intertwined with the soporific sound of the crowd's applause, provided the soundtrack to endless childhood summers in Surrey. When I wasn't outside playing cricket with my brother Mark, I would be watching Wimbledon with my mum. She is a keen tennis player, and Mark and I used to go along to the tournament together most years to watch. I loved the atmosphere and the thrill of seeing all those top players. A couple of summers ago I was given a pair of tickets to Wimbledon by the BBC for doing an interview with John Inverdale on Radio Five Live so I took Mum along. I watched Anna Kournikova; Mum spent her time checking out Newcombe and Roche.

Safely cosseted by these warming thoughts, I could have lain in that bed all day. Then the nurse came in. It was time. As the anaesthetist put the drip into my hand I asked if I should count down from 10 – I'd seen that on the TV before.

'Do you want to?' he said.

'No, I think I'll just . . .'

Later, I came round confused.

'Sorry, I must have dropped off there. When are we going in?' I asked the nurse.

'You've been in.'

That was that. I left the hospital a day later – someone asked if

I was Michael Owen on the way out – and recuperated for a while at my parents' house, watching the tennis.

Although I was in quite a lot of pain after the operation, I was desperate to fulfil a promise I had made myself beforehand to go on holiday. It was to be my first proper break in three years of professional rugby. My mum and dad have an apartment in Spain and I had planned a trip there with my brother, Mark, and a couple of friends. It was still early days after the operation but I really needed the space. I had to go.

At first everything seemed to be going fine – sun and swimming helped the healing process along well and I even managed some light jogging. Then my world was in danger of falling apart. A few days into the holiday I was eating dinner in a restaurant with my friends when I felt a burning sensation in my groin, like someone was pushing a hot poker into me. I couldn't lean backwards without being in agony. Hunching over the table, I carried on with the meal hoping the feeling would go away but when it came time to leave I could hardly stand up. What the other diners thought of four blokes helping a 21-year-old granddad to the door, I don't know. The guys had to bring the car to the restaurant entrance because I couldn't walk.

As I lay in bed that night with an icepack on my groin, I was afraid. All sorts of thoughts passed through my head. Had the operation gone wrong? Would I miss the start of the season? Would I miss the whole season? There was so much to look forward to – an exciting young Newcastle team, an England side who had beaten one of the southern hemisphere giants last time out and, of course, the race to make the Lions. It couldn't all be taken away like this – could it?

In trepidation, I phoned Jerry Gilmore in the morning and he told me to take things easy but reassured me that I would be fine. He was right. Gradually the pain eased and the healing process began once again. It had been a blip, albeit an alarming one. By the time the holiday ended, I was a long way down the road to recovery. I returned to England relieved, refreshed and raring to go for the start of a season unlike any other. The journey from Falcon to Lion had begun.

Out of

chapter two

Out of the blocks

The 2000–01 season was being billed, on Tyneside at least, as Newcastle's second coming. Having won the championship three years previously on the back of Sir John Hall's investment, the Falcons had almost become extinct when he pulled out and retired to Spain. But by then, Dave Thompson had arrived as the white knight to save the club and set it on the right track. He was another multi-millionaire but a rugby man through and through, and this time, rather than just signing ready-made star players, long-term foundations were being laid.

I could see the club's potential and despite enduring a fairly unsuccessful 1999–2000 season, it never crossed my mind to leave. I had signed a new two-year contract at Kingston Park and was looking forward to seeing what we could achieve. I cannot understand why sportsmen sign contracts they have no intention of fulfilling. Loyalty is an integral part of any team sport.

The first Premiership title had been won with a huge pack playing power rugby, which I had watched in some awe as an 18 year old, sometimes from the replacements' bench. This time, with a home-grown side, the director of rugby Rob Andrew and coach Steve Bates had decided on a different style. This modern approach involved all 15 players and much more movement, but we needed to be fit to pull it off successfully.

The new Zurich Premiership season was starting early – 19 August – to accommodate championship play-offs for the first time. By the end of September, the domestic season would already be a third over and with five of our first eight games at home, we needed a flying start. Time was short if we wanted to be ready.

Newcastle had brought back Steve Black, the larger than life conditioning coach who had originally come over to the Falcons from Newcastle United Football Club. Blackie, self-proclaimed love child of Pavarotti, part-time actor and scriptwriter, and ex-boxer, sprinter and footballer, had resigned from the conditioning job with the Welsh national side after ill-placed criticism over the fitness of some international players, and had returned to his native north-east. He was put in charge of preparing us. The Welsh players were upset when he left – they swore by him – and I was glad we were going to be able to tap into his expertise again, but I was concerned about what it might mean for my brother.

Mark, or Sparks as everyone calls him, had taken over as Newcastle's fitness conditioner when Blackie departed for Wales. Since he is also my housemate in rural Northumberland, there was inevitably a good deal of late-night speculation about what the future may hold.

Sparks and I have always been close. He is 17 months older than I am and we have done everything together. Living and working with him at Newcastle is an extension of the Wilkinsons' tight family bond. I trust his advice when it comes to training, particularly the fitness side, and I didn't want to lose him.

I needn't have worried. Newcastle made Sparks Blackie's right-hand man, giving him the responsibility of bringing on the next generation of talented young Falcons. It was good he was staying. I mean, who was going to do the washing-up otherwise?

Undoubtedly, Blackie was a shrewd addition to the staff. He is more than just a fitness coach; he is a psychologist and a shoulder to lean on. The final motivational words in the dressing room before a game often come from him. Bearing in mind his aura and personality, that can be very effective.

One of Blackie's many talents is writing the most obscure programme columns around. This is an example:

> Here's an interesting thing to do. Turn to a complete stranger and say, 'Hey, you there . . . yes, you. Take your hands from your pockets or I'll read you all the boring bits from Evelyn Waugh's *Brideshead Revisited*.' Then, even if they do remove their hands from their pockets, still read them those boring passages. You should see their faces.

See what I mean?

I wasn't surprised when Graham Henry signed him up for the Lions tour. He is relentlessly positive, has the respect of all the players and he's such an honest bloke you know he will give it to you straight. If you are cheating yourself by skimping on training, he'll tell you.

He works the players hard, never really setting specific goals in terms of repetitions but looking on impassively as you push your body to its limits. He has the priceless ability of making you feel terrible for half an hour but great for the rest of the day.

In his efforts to give us the edge we needed, Blackie introduced us to the Dynos, resistance machines that had the nasty habit of pushing back as hard as you pushed. The more effort you put in, the tougher it got. These beasts were a killer and put us all through agonies. They even reduced a couple of our squad to throwing up. George Graham's chuck was bad enough but Andrew Mower, our new signing from London Irish, spewed on the first-team pitch. He was left to clean it up with a small glass of water. It was something our groundsman Ray was not used to dealing with. Ray is part of the furniture at Newcastle, a real character but also something of a loose cannon. He often asks me if he looks more like Ian Rush, Thomas Castaignede or Luca Vialli. Given that he is particularly thin with a moustache the answer is pretty easy. Ray is a great help to me, sorting out kit and generally making life as comfortable as possible. I'll often be kicking at Kingston Park and he will come along on his mower and stop for a chat. He is part of the reason my sessions last so long. Throw in 20 minutes of mindless banter, totally incomprehensible to any passer-by, and it is bound to take some time.

Newcastle had been fantastic in telling me to take off as much time as I needed after the operation but I was keen to get back. The amount of rugby I have played already in my short career makes it seem strange if I'm not playing or training. After a week's solo work building my fitness up again and easing my groin back into action, I felt able to rejoin my team-mates in pre-season work. It was a relief to do so. I had enjoyed my month off but I didn't like the feeling of being behind schedule. My team-mates had already been put through their paces on Tynemouth beach and were being woken early for 6 a.m. runs around Whitley Park. The park runs were real efforts at that unearthly hour but at least the graft was done by the middle of the morning and we had the rest of the day to recover.

Pre-season training isn't like going back to school. That used to give me the Sunday night blues but this, despite the pain and vomit, is different. It is a chance to meet up with colleagues who, because of the lifestyle rugby players follow, tend to be your best friends as well. This is certainly the case with us. Newcastle are one of the friendliest clubs around. I don't know if it is because of our isolated geographical position but we are generally a very welcoming group.

Our nearest derby is at Rotherham, over two hours away, so we are used to spending long periods in each other's company. We have learnt to deal with all the travelling. The journeys allow us time to talk, laugh and generally enjoy being together. The team bus can be a vibrant place after a win and, despite professional puritanism, a few beers are allowed.

For some reason, Newcastle seems to attract people who are great characters as well as fine rugby players. Rob Andrew and coach Steve Bates are excellent judges of character and they aim to bring in not only good players but good people as well, among whom the following are some of the key characters.

Steve Bates is a genuine, down-to-earth guy. When Newcastle play well, Batesy is the main reason why. He has a strange habit, carried over from his scrum-half days, of licking his fingers. He coached me at Lord Wandsworth College back in Hampshire, and also taught me some pretty slack chemistry, no thanks to which I ended up getting an A at A-level. In his spare time, he's a golf buff.

Peter Walton is the forwards' coach. He had to retire from playing because of a neck injury. His family have a shop in Northumberland that sells great pies, and Peter supplies us with joints of meat from time to time. His nickname is Sgt Hightrousers because if he wore his strides any higher he could cut the pockets out for armholes.

Doddie Weir is the captain and a 1997 British Lion. As head of the fines committee and the players' lottery fund, he chooses the numbers and decides where our £5–10 goes each week. Since we never win anything, there are suspicions that it pays for Doddie's lavish lifestyle. One of the heavies on the fines committee is Richard Arnold, a hard-working flanker. He is known as F and C for his graphic use of the English language. His ginger-moggy hair turns gradually more yellow with each card he picks up. 2000–01 was his testimonial year.

Andrew Mower is a complete nutcase with a blatant disregard for his own safety. In his native Australia he's known as the Six Million Dollar Man because that's how much it would cost to put him back together. Shortly after he turned up at Newcastle from London Irish, he smashed a plate over his own head and needed stitches. Despite his heroism, he struggles to hold a decent conversation – in his own words, 'My chat stinks.'

Another new recruit to the back row, this time from Second Division Worcester, is solicitor Jim Jenner. He managed to let himself in for a season of ridicule when he stood up during his first team meeting – 'Hi . . . Jim Jenner,' he schmoozed in his cut-glass accent.

Gareth Maclure is a very tall, fast winger widely known as Girth McLength, and John Leslie, former Scotland captain, is nicknamed The Bogan, which is a none too complimentary way to describe a New Zealander. Despite claiming that offensive hair behind his ears on his passport photo was an unfortunately placed shadow, we convicted him of formerly sporting a mullet hairstyle. He's never lived it down.

Stuart Grimes is a very nice man from Scotland with the biggest feet I've ever seen, who obviously spends each Christmas with the Hendersons. An international second row, he wears tape around his head, which makes it look like a birthday cake although clearly without the candles.

Va'aiga Tuigamala, our devastating tackler and power runner capped by the All Blacks and Samoa, was once a special guest at a black-tie dinner where the Master of Ceremonies rightly introduced him as a rugby legend in both codes. 'He has,' gushed the MC, 'taken over the north east and is a name everyone knows and no one will forget. Ladies and gentlemen, please show your appreciation for Egu Tugumulu.' He's been called Egor ever after by the team. He prefers his usual shortened name, Inga.

George Graham, former Carlisle rugby league player turned aggressive Scottish international prop, is the only player to have his own reserved seat on the Falcons team bus apart from Wayne the driver. He believes backs training is a delicate balance between chatting and drinking tea. He is also responsible for Newcastle's semi-dance try celebration. Marius Hurter, the South African Test prop with a yearning to become a Geordie, has the dressing room in stitches with his ropy Ali G impression and even worse Biffa Bacon, out of the *Viz* comic. Gary Armstrong, former Scotland scrum-half, is known as the junkyard dog because he will play rugby whenever and wherever he can and never has a bad game. His Borders accent is occasionally impenetrable even to his fellow Scots, which can be difficult for his English half-back partner.

Liam Botham, our new signing from Cardiff, is equally talented in the centre or on the wing. He has a fantastic approach to training but takes a lot of stick for being a red-wine connoisseur aged 23. He also has the mickey taken by some for his regimented approach to diet, and by me for bringing his dog to kicking practice. He's called 'Son Of' by Egor, for obvious reasons.

Liam was the summer arrival everybody was talking about and he fitted in quickly. Being a Botham brings with it a lot of attention and in that respect coming to Newcastle was, I think, a good move for him. He was on the brink of signing for Harlequins but if he had gone to London, I'm sure the media spotlight would have been directed even more brightly towards him. Any sport in Newcastle is a comfortable second behind the local religion, football, so a rugby player is relatively anonymous. While Alan Shearer can't buy a Big Mac without being mobbed, Liam and I can eat out in the city without being pestered too much. Jonah Lomu could probably do the same.

The Falcons are growing, though. There are autographs to sign when I'm out and about and occasionally people sidle up to me and ask, 'Do you play for England?' to which I have yet to concoct a better reply than yes, 'sometimes'. Early in the season one girl did come up and pinch my bottom when I was in the cinema queue but that's as wild as the attention gets for rugby players up here.

Liam, who is married with children, was at Newcastle solely for the rugby and the Falcons squad soon found out what a dedicated trainer he is. He always wants to do that bit extra. No wonder he is so powerful. He may have chosen a different sport from his dad but he has certainly inherited the family's competitive gene, which was a plus for the team's card school. Pete Massey, the shark among the Falcons, was delighted.

The Botham card skills came to the fore on a team-bonding week in Narbonne. Rob had decided that a week in France would be the perfect tonic before the start of the new season and while we were there we drew up our aims for the coming months. Naturally we wanted to win every game but we put a special emphasis on qualifying for the Heineken Cup for the first time.

We had played at Narbonne in the European Shield the previous season and been impressed by their superb multi-sports complex which included running tracks, pitches and swimming pools. It was no holiday camp. There was training three times a day, starting at 8 a.m. with a skills session, then a weights work-out at 10.30 followed by a rest until 5 p.m. when we would get down to some rugby as a team. The hard graft we were putting in would pay off later, we hoped.

There wasn't much to do at night at the complex. This being the professional era, heavy drinking and wrecking hotels were out so we had to make our own entertainment. We were press-ganged into learning the words to the Geordie national anthem, 'Blaydon Races', by Doddie Weir, which was to come in handy later in the season. There was also some impromptu Polynesian dancing from Jamie Noon at the on-site restaurant. Some of the local Polynesians put on a performance at dinner and our South Sea Islanders, Inga Tuigamala and Epi Taione, joined in. They knew what they doing but Jamie, who is more of a North Sea islander having been raised in Whitby, was clearly making it up as he went along. Badly.

The card school was in full swing but I found myself involved in a splinter group playing Balderdash along with Stuart Grimes and Gareth Maclure. Burning the midnight oil playing board games – it's a crazy life being a rugby pro! Actually, midnight was out of the question. We were so tired that we were safely tucked up in bed by 9 p.m.

For all the hard work, it was a valuable trip. The time we spent together fostered a feeling of togetherness that it would not have been possible to achieve at home where players have their own lives and families. In France, it was just us and that was vitally important in becoming a family of our own. We returned convinced that all was well with the world. Then we had a warm-up match against Leeds and it was disastrous.

I went off with a dead leg but that was the least of the team's worries. Ross Nesdale and Jamie Noon both suffered concussion and were ruled out for three weeks; and Gary Armstrong fractured his cheekbone although the 'junkyard dog' decided he was fit to start the Premiership campaign anyway. We all had flashbacks of the previous season's desperate catalogue of bad luck and injuries. Here we go again, was the instinctive thought.

However, if we were going to be successful we had to be adaptable, and we just had to put the injuries to one side. The whole point of growing a squad was to have younger players who could be trusted to step in. The exposure they had been given the previous season might have been harsh on some occasions but I knew the experience would stand them in good stead. As we launched our season and our new black kit with a press day at Bamburgh Castle, I felt sure we would surprise a few of the 'experts'. The newspaper pundits had us down to finish in the bottom half of the table, some even as low as tenth. We knew we were better than that.

The usual suspects were being tipped for the Premiership – Leicester, Bath and Northampton, plus Saracens after their summer spending spree which had brought Tim Horan and Thomas Castaignede to England. I still needed convincing. They had invested heavily in big names before without reaping the rewards they had hoped for. Clubs need an intangible extra quality to succeed.

Wasps were my dark horses for the Premiership. If any team were capable of muscling their way into the established band of title challengers, I thought it must be Nigel Melville's side. I'd never understood why their success had been restricted to Cup competitions; they had good players in key positions – Lawrence Dallaglio and Alex King, for instance.

As for the Falcons, we had been handed a daunting start, facing European champions Northampton and Premiership title-holders Leicester in the first two weeks. But they were both home games and two wins would underline our potential. Getting off on the right foot was crucial.

In the end, we managed one out of two. Beating Northampton was testament to the spirit we had developed in France. We hung on for a 27–21 win despite 10 minutes of constant pressure from the Saints at the end. It was all hands to the pumps as wave after wave came at us. In their last attack, Pat Lam was pulled up for crossing – a referees' favourite during the early part of the season – and we were safe. We had spent quite a lot of time working on defence and its importance showed up straightaway.

The win was terrific but I couldn't help feeling concerned. If we needed to work that hard to take the points in every game it was going to be a long season. I desperately hoped the tackling side of my game wouldn't be needed so much. It's often when sides are fighting like mad to hang on that injuries occur. Rob Andrew had mentioned to me how important it was to look after my body but you can't go easy if your side is on the rack, defending a narrow lead. He had suggested using the forwards around me to carry the ball more instead of taking the punishment myself. Others told me to go easy on the big tackles. Self-preservation is a difficult attitude to take out on to a rugby field. I understand how important it is but I find it hard to alter my natural approach. I like to get involved early on and that can mean running into heavy traffic or clearing rucks and mauls. As for tackling, I enjoy it.

At least there were no concerns about my groin. I had been kicking as soon as the operation would allow and was relishing the chance to test everything in a competitive match. I was pleased to find all in working order.

Kingston Park presents a kicker with an unusual situation. We are on an exposed plain and it always seems to be windy, which is not ideal but adapting to the conditions is part of the challenge. In the Northampton game the wind blew across the field from the clubhouse, the opposite direction to usual. Doing your homework helps. I try to gauge how strong the wind is in pre-match practice and make my plans accordingly. The ball is affected only as it slows down, in the second half of its flight. So if I'm close in, I just aim straight; there is no need to allow for the wind. For longer-range kicks, I aim various degrees inside or, in extreme cases, outside one of the posts and allow the wind to do its worst. On this occasion, my calculations went OK and I managed to land six out of seven.

The scalp of the European champions was important for us psychologically and it set Northampton off on the wrong foot. They were knocked out of the Heineken Cup before Christmas. It was to take them a lot of effort and a long time to get into their stride.

The Kingston Park wind tunnel was a factor when we played Leicester. Tim Stimpson knew what to expect having played for Newcastle, but he had a tough time with his kicking, and to round off his day he left with a black eye courtesy of Richard Arnold. He was still smiling, though, because Leicester won 25–22. We probably bottled it after racing into a 13–0 lead. I don't think we could believe it and we ended up giving the champions too much respect, too much possession and the match.

The game was overshadowed by events off the pitch. Rob Andrew tore a strip off Leicester for their persistent ball killing and sparked a row that ran and ran in the press. Rob said that if everyone approached the game like the Tigers we might as well give up on professional rugby as a spectator sport. He was frustrated by what he saw as cynical slowing down of possession for which somebody should have been sin-binned. Rob singled out Leicester's England contingent – Martin Johnson and Neil Back – for special criticism and claimed referees were afraid to yellow card them because of who they were. Leicester were certainly happy to concede a penalty and three points rather than give us the quick ball we needed to attempt to score a try, but whether they were any more guilty than any other Premiership club is debatable. Let's face it – we all do it.

Everyone understands that if a side is able to gain speedy possession after a tackle, it gives them the chance to attack a disorganised defence. If you have players in your side who can slow the process down, it buys you time to sort yourselves out and be ready for the next wave of runners. Unless you do something to disrupt the attackers, you will spend all day going backwards. Sides can do this legitimately by challenging for the ball at the tackle – David Wilson at Harlequins is brilliant at this aspect of the game but he walks a tightrope a lot of the time. I can understand why he does it. There are occasions when you would be letting your side down if you didn't break the rules. I have done it and I would do it again.

Take our game against Gloucester in the middle of a hectic three-match spell the following week. I didn't cheat but afterwards I wished like mad I had done. It was a perfect example of how streetwise rugby pays. Joe Ewens scored the match-winning try late on from clean possession, when I should have killed the ball after making a tackle. I regretted it bitterly. We simply gave the Gloucester game away after being in total control. We knew we had the players to win it but mentally we just weren't switched on for the full 80 minutes. Gloucester pulled the match out of nowhere.

The 19–18 defeat was as frustrating in its own way as England's losses to Wales and Scotland in successive seasons that had denied us the grand slam. I don't remember much about games that go well, but

I do remember the other ones. Ask me about England's win in Bloemfontein and I wouldn't be able to recall much; ask me about the grand-slam defeat against Scotland at Murrayfield, or this game, and I can give you chapter and verse. That is where I draw my motivation. I'm determined never to make the same mistake twice.

I have trouble sleeping at night after a game at the best of times because of all the pent-up nervous energy but I couldn't get off until the early hours after Gloucester. I went over and over the match in my mind, thinking what I should have done in certain situations and how we should have won. We could not afford home defeats if we wanted to live with and become one of the big boys in the Premiership.

I try not to talk about rugby after a match and in that respect living with Sparks is great because he knows that. I usually switch off with some mind-numbingly boring television – late-night poker and golf tournaments are a favourite. Among our little luxuries are a huge TV in the living room in front of which are plonked a couple of super-comfy black leather armchairs. They have a built-in massage facility and provide a haven for mind and body after the stresses and strains of professional rugby. I do have a brain – I'd have gone to Durham University if rugby hadn't intervened – but the last thing I feel like doing after all that hard work is using it. Studying Kafka will have to wait, as will the sports psychology course I started and shelved; winding down from rugby does not give me time to do it justice.

Winding down from the Gloucester defeat took some doing. It was all the more frustrating because we had started this congested period well with an excellent win at Sale. They had set off fast with victories over Bath and Gloucester but we played some good rugby to see them off 27–13. There were promising signs that we could take the style we wanted to adopt from the blackboard on to the pitch. Heywood Road was our first experience of a hostile crowd at a place where we had taken a heavy beating the previous season and we showed a lot of character and worked hard for our win.

Sale also gave me my first direct experience of the new one-minute rule for goalkickers. It had been introduced to keep the game moving and restrict stoppages to a minimum. I had taken a knock in the build-up to one of our tries and was down on the ground when the conversion was due. The referee, John Barnard, came up and informed me the clock was ticking because the tee was on the pitch. Rushing to my feet, I asked him how long I had left. It was only when he told me I still had 45 seconds that I realised just how much leeway a minute gives a kicker. Until then I had felt paranoid that I would overshoot the minute at some point.

I modified my approach slightly because of the rule's introduction, cutting out any wasted time, but it plays into my hands anyway. The shorter time I take to kick, the more likely it is that I'm kicking well. Delaying the process causes doubts to surface in my mind. The longer the wait, the more agitated the crowd becomes as well, which makes the kick harder in itself.

The hangover from the Gloucester defeat would probably have lasted longer if the game hadn't come in the middle of such a hectic week. We were able to divert our anger into beating Rotherham four days later, which at least meant we finished the week in credit.

Playing three games in eight days is far from ideal but how you deal with midweek rugby is part of the challenge of professionalism – sponsors and employers have to be satisfied. However, the quality suffers when we try to cram in too many matches. It stands to reason that if you give people a week to fine-tune for a game as opposed to half a week, they will produce a better standard. Usually it takes me four days to prepare but with midweek games something has to give, probably practice.

There are also bumps and bruises to think about. Sports such as cricket, and basketball and baseball in the United States, are played virtually day in, day out but physically their demands are totally different from those of rugby. A better comparison is with American Football where they play around 16 games per season and each one is a big event for players and spectators alike. When you think that top rugby players could be involved in something like 40 matches with the tours at the end of the season, extra midweek games are not exactly welcome.

Next up was Bath. The match was played against a surreal backdrop. Petrol blockades across the country had put the fixture in doubt because Bath weren't sure their supporters would be able to get to the Rec. We were OK because we had booked a coach – and therefore some fuel – well in advance.

It was a strange time with the country almost paralysed by handfuls of peaceful protestors complaining about the price of fuel. For the Newcastle players, many of whom lived outside the city, travelling to training was a problem. George Graham had to come across the country from Carlisle and Gary Armstrong from Jedforest, across the border. I drove to training from my home 20 minutes away a lot slower than usual to try to conserve petrol – all the tractors were held up behind me. The Mercedes sportscar I had then wasn't the best for fuel economy but I must have been slightly over-cautious because I still had a third of a tank left when the blockade ended.

Bath, when we eventually reached the place, was a disappointment. Instead of trying to outplay them, we ended up fighting them, and another game against a top side slipped away. Mike Tindall's try proved decisive in a 19–12 defeat although it was a close call whether there was a double movement as he went over the line.

This was another game in which ball killing played its part. We were in trouble 25 metres from our own line so after I smother-tackled Shaun Berne, I lay on top of the ball on the floor. Inevitably, this sort of thing frustrates opponents and if you do it you have to accept what is coming to you. I took a lot of 'shoe' and a few punches from their forwards, but the ball was slowed up and we kept them out. The end justified the means, and you expect a bit of rough treatment if you do that.

Being rucked does hurt but if you can't handle it, you shouldn't be playing rugby. I remember taking a fearful amount of punishment for England 18-Group in our grand-slam game against Wales. It took place off the ball so it was out of order and the raw state of my back afterwards almost prompted our management to take a photo and send it to the Welsh with a complaint.

There are definite no-go zones and the head is one of them, or it should be. I'd taken a couple of boots to my head in pre-season against Leeds, which hadn't impressed me, and it happened again at Bath. I was competing for the ball on the ground with Iain Balshaw when someone came clattering in and accidentally caught me across my temple, eyes and bridge of the nose with his boot. This kicked off a big fight – players naturally get angry about careless footwork – which sort of summed up the entire match.

In the end, we opted to play for a point rather than the win. A new scoring system had been introduced over the summer, based on the southern hemisphere Super-12s, which gave a side one point for losing by a margin of seven or less. It was supposed to encourage sides to keep playing until the final whistle. Ten points down when we were awarded a penalty in the last minute, we decided to kick it rather than go for the try. It was the right call in the circumstances but an acknowledgement of defeat, which felt strange.

Even though most people would have expected us to lose, the Bath defeat was a setback. It put our home game against Wasps the following week into the critical category.

This match brought the return of Inga to the starting line-up. Our fearsome wing had endured a busy summer with Samoa and was carrying a couple of injuries so Newcastle had taken to using him as an impact substitute. Some impact – running into him should carry a health warning. In his place on the wing we had used Epi Taione. He was our own mini Inga, although at 6ft 4ins and 18st 4lb he wasn't exactly mini. In the beginning Epi was a little raw in some respects but his physical attributes are amazing – he always made yards when he returned the ball. It's no wonder New Zealand are such a force in world rugby when they can call on the South Sea Islanders. Having one of them in your team is a plus – imagine what it's like when half the side possesses that sort of power.

Despite Epi being a rival for his place, Inga took him under his wing, putting him up at his house until he found his feet after his move from local junior rugby. You wouldn't expect anything less of Inga, a committed Christian and an inspiring person to have around. Inga never rams his beliefs down our throats but if the conversation gets round to religion, he will talk about it to us. He always takes his guitar with him on away trips and plays it in his room.

He is held in enormous respect at Newcastle and everyone tries to watch their swearing around him, not always successfully. The number of team-talks that have been interrupted by the familiar words 'sorry, Inga' are countless. The way he lives his life makes him a great role model and ideal for helping to sow the seeds of rugby union around Newcastle.

The contrast between Inga off the field and Inga on it is total. Close up, his competitive face is a mask of evil when he is running at someone. Having him on your side is like possessing a 'get out of jail free' card. If you are in trouble, you know you can always throw Inga the ball and he will bale you out. It's important not to box him in by putting boundaries on what he is allowed to do – we've made that mistake from time to time. It is much better just to leave him to do what he feels is right. The odd occasion when he isn't where he should be is more than made up for by the damage he can do by cropping up where he wants.

Wasps were his old club and he duly made his mark by hitting Paul Volley with a murderous tackle that left him in a crumpled heap. They had crushed us the previous season at Kingston Park. How sweet it felt to turn the tables on them. We played to our potential in running up a half century against them. OK, the scoreline flattered us a little – Gary Armstrong's two late tries were gift-wrapped – but at times we were extremely dangerous with the ball in hand. As so often happens when you are attacking well, we left a few holes in defence and I missed a couple of kicks I should have landed, but we were delighted nonetheless.

Wasps were not so happy. Lawrence Dallaglio publicly accused some of the team of playing to their own agendas. They were eliminated from two Cup competitions before Christmas.

No one was under any illusions that such a convincing victory suddenly made us world-beaters, just as the home defeat against Gloucester hadn't made us relegation fodder. But there were plenty of plus points for the team in the way we had played, and also for me, for once, in putting over a 45 metre drop goal. It came off my weaker right foot, which was a vindication of a lot of hard work in training. I had been practising with both feet and for some reason was enjoying more success with the weaker one.

Having seen off Wasps, it was important we closed the first part of the Premiership season with a win at Harlequins. They had rebuilt their side completely over the summer and had got away to a sticky start so we felt we had a chance. Away wins were going to be elusive and this was an opportunity for us to pinch one.

The mention of a trip to Harlequins makes me feel queasy because of the balls they use. Quins like to use balls with their club colours on – magenta, French grey, chocolate brown, light blue, black and light green. Because of this, they use an old-style Gilbert ball rather than the newer ones most of the other clubs employ. They react differently when you kick them. I can never manage to get hold of any to practise with before we play there so I end up going to the Stoop cold and dreading it.

This time the kicking went well but as full time approached, the match was on a knife-edge. We were trailing 18–16 but were awarded a penalty and I was called up to have a shot at goal to win the game. It was five metres in from touch and 30 metres out but there was a slight cross-wind blowing.

'Earn your money, young 'un,' grunted George Graham, not particularly helpfully, as I went to line up the kick. I was about to kick a ball I feared and the devils in my head were in overdrive, but I cast them to one side and went through my familiar routine.

The first point is to set up the ball correctly. Each type has its own sweet spot – even the Quins version – and the aim is to make sure the ball is placed in a position that will ensure you can make contact with it every time. With the ball leaning slightly to the left, I take four steps back and then five across to the right, then one step in to the ball. This is an invariable part of my routine.

At the end of my run-up I tense my left foot and bend it downwards while visualising and feeling where on my foot I want to strike the ball. I find a point I want the ball to travel to – at Quins it was just inside the left-hand post because of the cross-wind – and then, when I'm happy, I trace an imaginary line back to the ball from that point. The idea is for the ball to travel along that trajectory as if it were travelling along a wire. I approach the ball carefully, focusing exactly on the part that I'm going to strike, and with a straight swing of the left leg the ball is on its way. I hold the position afterwards as it heads for the posts.

The mechanics need to be correct, but at the same time I have to be comfortable within myself. State of mind is as important as technique; success or failure is governed by feel as much as anything. Most times, I know whether I've kicked a goal as soon as I've struck the ball. There is no need to look.

This time, because of the wind and ball, I wasn't sure. I hit it well and the ball drifted back on the wind as planned. For a moment I was concerned it would come back too far but between the posts it went and after one more play the referee blew for the end of the game. I had earned my money.

In the dressing room afterwards, Rob told us to enjoy the moment but stressed we hadn't played all that well and would need to improve our performances. We knew that but, with a long journey to Newcastle ahead, it was just what the doctor ordered. The mood is always so much better after a win. After away games close to home, some players will often sip a few beers on the team bus on the way back and then make a night of it in Newcastle. However, a victory at a place like Quins is always tempered by the length of the return journey. As it was we had a few laughs, a few games of cards and watched a film but there was no serious partying.

This Newcastle team is more restrained than its predecessor. I remember one trip back from a game in London a couple of years ago which degenerated badly. As the drink flowed, a challenge was set to swing from the back of the bus to the front, using only the overhead luggage racks as support. Naked, in one case.

I opted out but didn't escape entirely as I had my favourite boxer shorts removed and thrown out of the bus. There was no repeat this time. Instead we reflected on what we had achieved so far.

That narrow win meant we had completed the first chunk of the Premiership season in third place. There had been frustrations along the way but if someone had offered me a top-three spot after our loss at Bath, I would gladly have taken it. The Falcons were airborne again.

chapter three

England calling

Although all my efforts had been concentrated on Newcastle's Premiership programme, England had never gone away. The national squad management and I had kept in contact throughout the whole period.

We had all received a letter at the start of the season, including a breakdown of how we had fared on our summer tour with input from the various coaches. Mine was positive, saying how I had come on and encouraging me to keep developing. It stressed the importance of thriving on my role as a decision-maker rather than being pressurised by it. I agreed with the sentiments – I play a lot better when I'm relaxed and enjoying myself.

The letter also detailed a few training tips and the schedule for the coming weeks. That entailed setting aside half a dozen Mondays to travel down to our base at the luxurious Pennyhill Park Hotel in the Surrey countryside to train together as a squad. The idea was to make sure we remained as a team when we met up for the autumn international series and were not a bunch of club players thrown together a week before facing the world champions. It meant making an extra effort when we were tired after weekend matches but I wholeheartedly agreed with the plan. If the time was there, why not use it to try to keep up with our international rivals, many of whom spent nearly all of the season in each other's pockets?

I was determined to be as well prepared as I could possibly be for the back-to-back games against Australia, Argentina and South Africa, and the best way of doing that was being with England. Besides, I was excited at meeting up with the team again. The previous occasions had been happy times and I couldn't wait to see everyone.

The manager, Clive Woodward, was keen to introduce the next generation of internationals to the way we did things, so he included a development squad in our Monday training sessions. That meant some company on the flight down from Newcastle as Liam Botham, Jamie Noon, Michael Stephenson and, later on, Dave Walder were all involved. I was made the Falcons representative, which meant having to coordinate their movements. We were allowed to miss one session after a European Shield trip to Bordeaux but other than that, attendance was compulsory.

During the summer we had all been supplied with precise fitness plans worked out by Dave 'Otis' Reddin, the RFU's conditioning coach. These were different for each player. Guys like Jason Leonard obviously concentrated more on strength while someone like Dan Luger probably had explosive speed at the top of his list of priorities. It was up to each individual to specify what areas they needed to concentrate on. Mine was an all-round plan with the emphasis on improving my power and size. I'm not the biggest player in the side and muscle building is important in what is a highly physical environment. In practical terms, it meant consuming a lot of protein milk shakes, and including plenty of meat and egg whites in my diet. I used to think I was eating healthily by having cereals in the morning but I was advised also to have egg-white omelettes to try to bulk myself up.

The fitness plans were supposed to help us peak for the autumn internationals but that presented a problem. We had Newcastle's training schedule to deal with as well. Otis's methods were different from Steve Black's – they set down more precise routines for every exercise – and while they were equally valid, doing both would have tired me out. I wanted to be at my best for Falcons' games as well as England's and I could see potential difficulties if I overloaded myself. I took on board all the England advice and chose predominantly to follow Newcastle's plans, occasionally combining the two. Working under an acknowledged expert such as Blackie was preparing me well for England in any case, and Otis was well aware of this. The way I approach rugby, my next game is my biggest and that applies equally to club and country.

While the other Falcons would take a taxi to the team hotel from the airport when we arrived at Heathrow on a Sunday night, I was picked up by my dad and spent the night at my parents' home, which is only 15 minutes away from the hotel. I found the normality of seeing them a good way to switch off from the pressures of professional rugby. Once I was through the front door, I was in a different world. Staying over at Mum and Dad's gave me the chance to catch up not only with them but also with my sleep. I was able to relax with a much-appreciated lie-in before meeting up with the squad at 10 o'clock on Monday morning.

I'm still very much a family person. I suppose I was pretty easy to parent – I wasn't much of a teenage rebel. Some weeks I speak to my dad every day, which may be a little unusual at my age but I'm quite at ease with it. I seek his advice on a lot of issues. It makes sense since he has a lot more experience in life than I have and, in any case, we're very much on the same wavelength.

Dad and I have a two-tiered relationship. He takes a day off a week from his job as a financial adviser to help look after my off-field affairs. He knows about the business side and, equally important, he knows about the rugby side too, having played county rugby for Somerset. Nothing is allowed to intrude into my training, however lucrative it might be.

As far as I was concerned, the most important point of these Monday training sessions was the personal element rather than technical advancement. Keeping us bonded together as a team was vital if we were to beat the southern hemisphere sides. We clicked straight back into the summer-tour mentality with plenty of gossip and banter exchanged between the players.

The squad's 'characters' are Austin Healey and Phil Greening. Austin is a bit of a joker and very good to have around for morale's sake. When I first arrived at an England squad session as a nervous teenager, he asked me if I was one of the competition winners who occasionally got to warm-up with the team and whether I had my homework with me. He has always, without fail, got something to say, and it is usually amusing.

Phil (the 'blob', as the *Sun* called him) has the gift of the gab too but uses it for other purposes. His dates during the season included – again according to the *Sun* – the pop singer Natalie Imbruglia before he settled down and got himself a steady girlfriend. He must be the only international rugby player who wears a tongue stud.

The player I find myself drawn quite close to is Ben Cohen. He is my age to start with, and a good, level-headed bloke. He was depicted as being arrogant in some quarters after his 'Shane who?' comment. In fact he wasn't certain if he was being asked about winger Shane Williams or Shane Howarth, the former Wales full-back. He ended up upsetting the Welsh, but he isn't like that at all. I often find myself in the team room at Pennyhill Park idly knocking pool balls around with him. I also find Mike Catt good to talk to. Given the things he has been through and put up with in his career, he comes at everything from a unique perspective.

I'm a film fan and my DVD partner in the squad is Richard Hill, who is much better at picking decent movies than I am. Hilly leads Will Greenwood and Mike Tindall on the Thursday night cinema trip ahead of an international. Hilly could moan for England – or that's how the rest of the squad like to see it. Whatever he says gets thrown back in his face in a whining voice and he is so accustomed to it by now that it just washes over him.

The captain, Martin Johnson, is a funnier bloke than you might imagine from the famous frown – he balances light moments with the serious stuff. He is one of the boys rather than some distant figurehead and that sets the tone for the squad. Everyone is encouraged to contribute. Just having him around is a tremendous confidence boost to any team-mate.

Johnno is also the squad quiz king and often leads the Leicester contingent, plus myself and Joe Worsley, in a game we have devised. You jot down the numbers one to 26, assign two letters of the alphabet to each and then everyone has to name a famous person whose initials begin with those letters. The aim is to be original – if someone else has the same person, you miss out – and despite all those blows to the head, Johnno is exceptional.

We are quite a well-established squad by now and know each other well. We get along as a group, which helps. Once you have been through it a few times on the field together, you become friends almost by default. When I first came into the squad it was not as welcoming a place as it is now and because I'm shy I found it difficult. I ended up keeping myself to myself. Apparently I had it easy compared with players a few years earlier. However, Clive Woodward set about creating an environment where new players would feel comfortable and able to offer their opinions. I feel like I can say what I like when I like these days. There is no hierarchy.

The England players have a set of ground rules from the RFU under which we operate. The code of conduct ranges from banning mobile phone use during team meetings and in public areas (Newcastle have the same system which cost our owner Dave Thompson £100 when his went off in the changing room) to congratulating players who are selected ahead of you. Alcohol isn't even mentioned. It is taken as read these days that players know not to overdo it.

There is also no mention of stripping off for the camera so in October the England squad decided to pose for a calendar. It was titled 'Raw Talent' and ended up raising more than £200,000 for charity. While most of the team willingly bared all for a selection of tasteful pictures, I insisted on protecting my modesty. Ripping my kit off for the cameras really isn't me. The photographer wanted a shot of me lining up a goalkick at Twickenham with nothing on. No chance. The RFU conduct regular tours of the stadium – just imagine what those people would have thought.

'That's the South Stand and over there is the tunnel where the players run out . . .'

'What's that in the middle of the pitch?'

'Oh, that's just Jonny, naked, practising his kicking.'

I was pressured a little into taking off my shirt and posing for a press-up on the front cover of GQ *Active* and since then everyone seems to want me to disrobe. No less a sportsman than Lennox Lewis had been on the cover the previous month so when they asked, after a lot of trouble, I said yes. You live and learn.

The England management were sympathetic to our club commitments during our Monday sessions and they did not work us too hard. A lot of the guys couldn't do much physical work anyway because of injuries so there was plenty of tactical training, often split between backs and forwards, all geared towards our first game of the season against Australia.

We were trying to pick up where we left off against South Africa in the summer. No stone had been left unturned to make sure we were up with the competition. Clive had spent part of the summer with the Denver Broncos American Football team as well as Agen in

France, looking at their coaching methods. One of his strengths is his openness to new ideas.

Like me, he is a big fan of rugby league and, having already appointed former Great Britain coach Phil Larder as defence coach, he invited Ellery Hanley along to help out in the same area, with an eye on the summer tour to North America. Clive also called up Jason Robinson to the development squad before he had even played a game of rugby union for Sale. Jason's transfer from Wigan rugby league had caused quite a stir.

Being a fan of Jason's, I was keen to have a word with him when he turned up at Pennyhill Park. I may have come on a bit strong – I think he thought I was an autograph hunter. We talked about Wigan and the rugby league World Cup, which he chose to miss in order to move to union, and he told me how he was enjoying his new life and settling down well at Sale.

I was certainly impressed on the field. He seemed very devoted and keen to learn, and turned a few heads in training with his pace when he hunted down Iain Balshaw who is no slouch himself. Jason didn't look at all like a fish out of water. There was no doubt he was a very talented athlete and a superb runner. Time would tell whether he was able to adapt to union's idiosyncrasies.

First, there was the question of the kicking game, which has a much higher priority in union than in league. However blessed a runner he was, there were inevitably going to be occasions when Jason would be forced to kick from deep. Then there was the contact situation. Releasing the ball and presenting it well to your team-mates when you are tackled is imperative in union whereas in league Jason could use his wonderful running skills as he wished because there was no contest for the ball when he was tackled. His way of thinking had to be different in union. There is no point heading for the open spaces if no one is there to win the ball when you are brought down.

There was always the possibility that he could beat everybody. He has such a talent it would be wrong to put too many restrictions on him. It was probably best for his team-mates to adapt to his style and try to second guess where he was headed. His involvement in our training sessions suggested England were at least willing to consider that option.

Mondays with England also represented a chance for me to brush up on my kicking technique. I would always finish off by having a stint with Dave Alred, the team's specialist coach in that area, before catching the evening flight back to the north east. Dave is the man who helped Rob Andrew become such a fine kicker. I speak to him regularly during the season, checking everything is going smoothly with my kicking. We have worked together for five years now and although my routine is my own, the principles of it were developed through working with him. The time I've spent with Dave makes it easier for me to work out why something has gone wrong and iron out any glitches on my own during matches.

Between sessions, the team kept in contact with the coaches, bouncing ideas off each other for the matches ahead. Often this involved using e-mail, which worked well enough until I lent my lead to Matt Perry and it disappeared back to Bath, never to be seen again.

Clive's reputation for being an e-mail buff had been criticised in some quarters, particularly by Richard Cockerill during his time with England. I quite liked it as a communication tool. The last thing I wanted to do when I was back in Newcastle was indulge in in-depth conversations over the phone about specific issues. It was much easier to send a considered reply on the computer. Richard Cockerill's point was that players should not find out they had been dropped via a computer screen, but ever since I have been involved with England, the news has always been delivered face to face. When I was left out of the 1999 World Cup quarter-final against South Africa, Clive took me to one side before announcing the team and went through his reasoning. I obviously disagreed but I had an inkling it was coming and I couldn't have asked for anything more than that.

As the first international of the autumn approached, I took time out to watch the Wallabies on television against the Scots. Usually I turn the television off if rugby union comes on when I'm trying to relax, otherwise I find myself analysing everything, but this was business. Plenty had been written about them being at the end of a long, hard season and under-strength in the absence of Steve Larkham and George Gregan, but there didn't seem to be much wrong with them at Murrayfield. We knew from bitter experience how difficult it was to win there but they were extremely professional in the way they wore the Scots down before pulling clear to win 30–9. It was going to be a tough assignment.

The week of 18 November did not start well. We gather on Sunday nights ahead of England matches but for some reason the RFU had booked me on to the wrong flight. If I had taken it, I would have turned up at Pennyhill Park a day late. When we discovered the error it was too late. As luck would have it, the rail chaos after the Hatfield crash, and the floods, meant every other flight from the north east was fully booked.

I spoke to Nathan Martin, the RFU's liaison man, and we agreed the best way around the situation was to travel down by road – so I grabbed the nearest willing taxi. A red Ford Sierra duly turned up on Sunday evening to collect me. I put my kit and my golf clubs in the boot, slid into the back and settled in for the journey. Setting off at 7 p.m., I knew I would arrive in Surrey fairly late but the route was simple – A1, M25, M3 – and the roads should have been clear at that time. I expected to be in bed by midnight at the latest.

I spent the first part of the trip phoning some friends on the mobile to kill some time, and chatting to my driver, an amiable Geordie. After a while my conversation wore a little thin so I decided to catch up on some sleep. I woke up at midnight. We weren't at Pennyhill Park. It was dark but this was definitely not leafy Surrey – it was far too built up for that. I had a look at some neon signs and discovered, to my surprise, that we were in Tottenham, North London. This wasn't part of the plan. Unfortunately, the driver didn't appear to be too well acquainted with the south of England – in fact I don't think he'd ever been there – and wasn't too well acquainted with a map, either. He didn't have one.

We stopped at a petrol station and I asked for directions, but following them made matters worse. By now we were in the middle of London. We tried a police station but they were so busy we walked back out again and decided to plough on. The situation picked up when we found some signs for the M25 and eventually, to our great relief, we met up with the London orbital. We were at junction 26, diametrically opposite where we needed to be.

There was a short debate about which way round we should go – it didn't really matter because it was about the same distance either way – and with that decided, I nodded off again. I woke up at 2 a.m. as we came off the M25 and on to the M3. Fifteen minutes later we were at the hotel. The journey had taken seven and a quarter hours. The fare came to £400.

The hotel paid it – they were reimbursed later by the RFU – and the taxi driver, who by now I knew like a brother, headed off back to Newcastle. I felt a bit sorry for him, thinking he wouldn't get back until 8 a.m. but this was tempered by the knowledge that he wouldn't have to work for a week. I thought about tipping him but the best tip I could come up with was 'buy a map'.

It wasn't the ideal start to the challenge of facing the world champions. I didn't hurry out of my bed on Monday morning and when I did get up I hit a few golf balls on the hotel course to work the horrendous journey out of my system. The best medicine was a good training session with the team at Twickenham that evening. We all had dinner together at the hotel and by Tuesday morning I felt human again.

After the official team announcement the next day, we went to meet the press. The main talking point was Ben Cohen's selection on the wing ahead of Austin Healey. Ben had missed part of Northampton's Heineken Cup campaign because of an incident in which his father was seriously assaulted in a nightclub, but he had returned to play some great rugby. Ben was obviously in high demand at the press conference and was telling the journalists how his father was out of intensive care and improving. Then, near the end of the session, Clive Woodward came in and had to tell him the news that his father had suffered a relapse and died. It was an awful situation.

I felt desperately sad for Ben. In some ways, this bolt out of the blue seemed more cruel because it had followed hot on the heels of such good news. I couldn't imagine how he felt. Matt Dawson, his close friend who had been selected on the bench, drove Ben back up to Northampton to be with his family. We all decided to wear black armbands for the anthems before the match as a mark of respect.

Life had to go on and we trained as normal with Austin taking Ben's place. Clive kept the position open but said he needed to know for definite if Ben would be able to play by Friday morning. In the end, Ben dropped out because although he felt his father would have wanted him to play, he said he couldn't risk letting the side down by not having his mind fully on the job.

For the rest of us, as the game drew nearer the nerves increased. Nathan Martin had been monitoring the weather forecast all week and pinning up reports in the team room. This earned him the unwanted tag of Michael Fish but his efforts revealed useful information. We were headed for the wettest winter on record and it looked like being a rainy and windy Saturday. With that in mind, we came up with a game plan that we felt would put them under pressure.

In the past, with Matt Burke at full-back, putting up the high ball was a waste of time – he could catch them in his sleep – but with

Burke on the wing, we wanted to test their new full-back, Chris Latham. We felt he could be vulnerable.

Burke's presence in the side meant they had a world-class goalkicker so we reckoned it was vital to play the game in their half to keep him out of range. That meant a kicking game from our territory for me. The rugby we wanted to play, we could save for their half.

We knew their defence would be good – they had a big backline and were very well organised – so we varied our tactics to include cross-kicks for our wingers to chase, as an attacking ploy.

It was important not to allow the larger and heavier Australian backs to dominate us. If they had the feeling they were going forward early on, they would run all over us. Those first tackles were going to be crucial – we had to put them on the floor.

My opposite number was Rod Kafer, who was not as well known as Steve Larkham but a classy player nonetheless. I was aware of what he liked to do but there was no point concentrating too much on a specific opponent – during the course of the game, you could end up one on one with anybody.

For me, Australia represented special opposition and not only because of their status as world champions. They had inflicted a 76–0 drubbing on us in Brisbane back in 1998. I swore at the time that I would try to learn from that experience so that it never happened again. I had played against them once since then, in the Centenary Test when we lost again, albeit a lot more narrowly. Now, as World Cup holders and Tri-Nations champions they were deservedly labelled the best team in the world.

As the game drew closer, I was aware of my kicking length increasing. This always happens before an international. It must be to do with adrenaline I suppose, but my body seems to gain extra strength from somewhere. By matchday Dave Alred was chasing all over Twickenham fetching the balls. Kicking practice had gone exceptionally well up to this point – I hadn't really missed anything – but on the morning of the game when I practised at the hotel, things started to go awry. It was windy and the kicks suddenly started to sway. I became very annoyed with myself. I couldn't work out whether it was the wind affecting the ball or the way I was striking it that was to blame.

I was preoccupied on the team bus and after a quick flick through the programme in the Twickenham dressing room, I put on my shorts and socks and went out for another kicking session. There was nothing unusual about this but after what had happened earlier it was important for my peace of mind that things went smoothly in my last rehearsal. Fortunately, they did. When everyone else had left the pitch, I took one more kick from in front of the posts to reassure myself. I always do this – if it doesn't go very well, I take another – and over it went.

I returned to my spot in the changing room. Our places are marked by a personalised nameplate. When players' international careers are over, these are given to them by the RFU. A couple of seasons ago Austin Healey's was pinched and mailed back to him. His Leicester team-mates were prime suspects.

A timetable is always pinned up on the changing room wall to make sure everything goes like clockwork. We should be finished getting ready 10 minutes before kick-off; on go the shoulder pads, then the England shirt, which is hanging up in the dressing room when we arrive. Dressed in pristine England white, I put adhesive on my hands to help grip the ball, then I smear some vaseline on top of my left ear. It split when I was 17 and is susceptible to cuts when I tackle – I've had it stitched three or four times. The only alternative is to wear tape around it, which looks faintly ridiculous with short hair. I don't wear a gumshield, although I should.

The nerves begin to grip as the time approaches. I find myself walking around the changing room, shaking my legs and generally fretting. I make myself sit down and compose my thoughts. With five minutes left, the management often leaves the room and there are just the 15 of us left. The substitutes are in the tunnel outside. We pull ourselves into a huddle, arms linked around each other's shoulders. Martin Johnson, Lawrence Dallaglio and Neil Back often say a few words, reminders mainly of what we have worked on all week and what we are in this for. Everyone chips in with the odd comment. There is no head banging, no screaming and no patriotic fervour. If a player isn't up for a game by now, he must either be totally devoid of emotion or dead.

The touch judge or fourth official comes in to tell us there are two minutes to go. As a last check, I visualise what I'm going to do in the game. Physically, I'm on fire, ready for what lies ahead; mentally, I try to remain ice cold. The last thing you need in an international is to have your thought processes clouded by red mist. I am desperate to get out on the pitch. It's a relief when the call comes from the referee and it's time to go.

The dressing-room door opens and out we come into the short tunnel. I'm in the middle of the line where I like to be. The pitch beckons a few metres away. We trot straight into a wall of noise. The sheer scale of Twickenham is what strikes you as you come out. The stands tower so high all around that you have to tilt your head backwards to see the sky. Some people say the stadium lacks atmosphere – not at that moment, they couldn't be further from the truth; 72,500 cheering spectators make a deafening noise. It's a wonderful feeling. I jog out on to the pitch but as soon as I reach the turf I slow down to a walk. Calmness is the state of mind I am searching for and this helps achieve it.

We line up for the anthems. If anything reminds you of just how lucky you are to be in this position, this is it. How many people would give their right arm to swap places at this moment? As 'God Save The Queen' reverberates around the stadium, the Sky television camera works its way along the line, focusing on each of us in turn. I try to ignore it and search for my dad in the crowd. I know my mum isn't always there – she gets so worked up she usually can't watch. She ended up spending an entire Six Nations match in a Twickenham bookshop once, before being spoken to by the store detective.

As I look out into the sea of faces I'm thinking about the game and I mumble rather than bellow the words to the anthem. The music ends to a huge cheer and rapturous applause. Finally, the game begins. England versus Australia – let's go.

Our forwards dominated possession from the start and I tried out Latham early on with some high balls but he handled them very well. We kept them pinned back but every time they escaped into our half, Burke seemed to land a penalty. He was kicking well considering the conditions. It was the first time I had known the ball to be blown about mid-flight at Twickenham and I missed a couple of kicks that I thought I had struck well. Nevertheless, half-time came with us 12–9 up. The message in the dressing room was that we were doing the right things and that if we kept doing them we would win.

The second half began badly. Three minutes into it, Burke went over for a try after Joe Roff had handed off Austin. Ten minutes later we conceded a penalty, which Burke put over. We were left one player short in defence when Austin had to fill in at full-back after Matt Perry had gone down injured. We pulled ourselves together and as the clock ticked on we were still in the match, trailing 19–15. Never once in those dramatic last few minutes did I doubt we were going to win. There was no panic. We had not played as well as we wanted to but importantly we had the territorial advantage and that was the key to the game. We kept pushing and probing, patiently trying to work an opening in their 22 and eventually, eight minutes into injury time, it came.

Latham was one of two Australians in the sin-bin so the Wallabies decided to play without a full-back for the closing stages, using their scrum-half Sam Cordingley as a sweeper instead. We spotted this and thought a chip through could bring rewards. Iain Balshaw, on as a substitute, delivered the kick in injury time and Dan Luger was up quickest to touch down. It was a try – or was it?

On the morning of the game, in my *Daily Express* column, I had written about the video referee being used for the first time at Twickenham and the impact it could have. That must've been clairvoyance. Referee Andre Watson called for video assistance to rule on Dan's try. There was a certain irony here because Andre had been the man in the TV booth in South Africa in the summer when Tim Stimpson's 'try' had been controversially ruled out in the first Test, a game we narrowly lost. This time Brian Stirling was the man studying the replay. I went up to Andre and asked him if there would be any play after the decision.

'Whatever happens, it's the end of the game,' he replied.

I felt helpless, knowing there was nothing any of us could do to alter the outcome. All we could do was wait. But as soon as I saw the replay on the giant screen, I knew. It was a try – we had won. There was a long delay while it was looked at from different angles and then the roar went up. The conversion did not matter in terms of the result but I wanted to finish the game on a high and, with the help of a verse from 'Swing Low' from the crowd, managed to put the kick over from the touchline. Cue final whistle and an ecstatic leap for joy.

People said the Wallabies were tired but, having been in their position over the summer in South Africa, I know just how much they would have wanted to end their season with a victory.

To turn a game we could have won against a top side into a game we did win was an important step in our development. It was a happy dressing room as our achievement sank in – we had beaten the world champions and everyone wanted a piece of us.

On the surface all looked well but in the background dark clouds had been gathering and the storm was about to break. English rugby was about to be thrown into turmoil on one of the most dramatic days in the game's history.

chapter four

Everybody out

They were only scraps of paper in an ashtray but they were dynamite as far as English rugby was concerned. The votes in the secret ballot to decide on strike action were unanimous. One word was scrawled on each piece of paper – yes. The England squad was withdrawing its labour for the Argentina game. We had come to the end of our tether. We could not agree our contracts with the RFU so we had decided to take the last and most drastic course of action left to us.

How it had come to this must have been hard to fathom for anyone on the outside, particularly as the sums involved were relatively small. But it was the culmination of more than a year's stalled negotiations that had frustrated the players and threatened to distract them from the business of playing rugby.

I first became aware of the difficulties during the World Cup when an issue over our intellectual property rights, that is the use of the players' images, cropped up. The rights had been sold by the RFU to its sponsors. The problem was they weren't the RFU's to sell; they belonged to us as individuals. When it came to drawing up contracts after the World Cup, these rights became a sticking point and a year later it still had not been sorted out.

There was also a problem with pay. The RFU wanted the majority of our income to be performance-related. They said a higher proportion of our money should come in win bonuses rather than match fees. The players saw that as unfair owing to the amount of effort we were putting in. No one could say we hadn't given every last drop of sweat in beating Australia but if the video ref's decision had gone the other way we would have lost. The way the RFU wanted things, something as random as that would have affected our livelihoods.

It wasn't just the financial and contractual issues that rankled with us; it was also the general impression that we weren't being treated properly by the RFU.

These negotiations seemed to have been going on for ever. In every game we'd put our bodies on the line, as you would expect us to do for our country, only to find nothing had changed. The England squad wanted all this out of the way so we could concentrate on playing, but the issues refused to go away.

Concerns had reached a critical level before the Australia game – we had no structure in place for being paid to play the world champions. As matters came to the boil, the contract business became harder and harder to ignore. Around the hotel, it was being mentioned all the time by the players. After each team meeting Johnno, who was conducting the negotiations on our behalf along with Matt Dawson, Lawrence Dallaglio and our agents CSS Stellar, would update us on progress – or the lack of it. It seemed we had to do something to make the RFU sit up and take notice so we could sort everything out once and for all. There was talk about turning our shirts inside out for training so when the photos appeared in the next day's papers, the sponsors' logos would be nowhere to be seen. We went against this course of action because our argument was not with the sponsors but with the RFU.

The decision was taken to shelve any action until after the Australia game and then consider a range of options, including strike action. If we beat the best side in the world, surely Twickenham would be sympathetic to our position.

We reconvened at Pennyhill Park for the Argentina match with spirits high. On the face of it, nothing seemed different. Kyran Bracken was the butt of all the jokes after falling for one of Austin's gags at lunch on Monday. Austin told whoever cared to listen that Martin Corry had a dog called Minton who had been in trouble recently when it had swallowed two shuttlecocks. 'Bad Minton,' said Austin. Everybody laughed including Kyran who then proceeded to quiz Martin Corry over what kind of dog Minton was. Kyran was roundly abused, told he was 'a bloody nice bloke', after Harry Enfield's Tim Nice-but-dim character, and immediately re-christened Minton. Bubbling away, though, was the more pressing issue. The players' representatives entered lengthy talks that evening with the RFU, which we knew would be decisive.

My dad was away in Australia so while they were talking I spoke to Rob Andrew and asked his advice. He told me that Newcastle would back me all the way if the England players decided to strike. He felt sure that no Premiership players would be released to fill our places if we pulled out of the Argentina game. This was reassuring news.

I was in my room when the call came at about 9 p.m. Johnno wanted to see us all downstairs. It took a while to contact everyone around the hotel complex but eventually all the players, plus CSS, were gathered in one of the meeting rooms. The atmosphere was tense. We all sat down and listened as Johnno informed us that the RFU were still refusing to budge. The talks had broken down again. It was decision time. We were asked for our thoughts. Should we strike or not?

The discussion lasted for two hours. We all gave our opinions, from the older players to the young ones, and voiced our fears. A lot was at stake and the meeting became quite emotional at times. I told everyone that all I had ever wanted as far back as I could remember was to play for England. I worked hard every day to make sure I had the chance to do so. By threatening to strike I would be putting it all at risk. But it was also pointed out – and I agreed – that if we did nothing we would never get anywhere; we would never receive a fair reward for all our graft. Rugby players have a short shelflife and we take a risk every time we go on the pitch and that fact needed to be recognised.

When everyone had been given their chance to have their say we voted. I wrote on my piece of paper, put it in the ashtray with the rest and Matt Dawson totted the votes up. We were on strike. I rang Rob to tell him the outcome and went to bed wondering what the next day would bring. I had a fair idea.

We had dropped a bombshell and when Clive Woodward heard about it he was upset. He arranged a meeting with us all at which things inevitably got a little heated and we were asked to leave the team hotel. We were told to check out and get away for a while. Clive had been involved all the way through the discussions and he felt that we had been given a good offer by the RFU. He also made it clear how he felt about using the England jersey to achieve our ends.

When the press arrived for the usual Tuesday morning gathering with the players, they discovered there weren't any. Instead, Clive and Francis Baron gave the RFU's side of what was developing into a huge story. At the same time, the players put together a statement via CSS to try to explain why we had acted in this way. It read as follows:

Extraordinary developments in the world of rugby have come to a head with the news that protracted negotiations between the RFU, the players and their representatives have broken down resulting in the England international rugby squad reluctantly but unanimously withdrawing from the game on Saturday.

[The decision] was taken following frustrating and inconclusive negotiations with chief executive Francis Baron during which the players sought an acceptable remuneration package including bonus and ticket allocations for international squad appearances.

The players are adamant that they have made every attempt to avert this situation and stress that they are prepared to play in the international this Saturday with no commercial tie-ins so this could be discussed at a later date. The honour of representing their country would far outweigh any commercial considerations but the players fear that the RFU are determined to stick with a stance which the players view as archaic.

The issue here from the players' side is one of principle and their main drive is to bring the sport into the 21st century and ensure that as performers they get something approaching a fair deal to bring them in line with other sports.

Most rugby players earn an annual salary commensurate with many Premiership soccer players' weekly drawings so there is no question of greed being a factor here. Rather, it is a case of challenging the RFU's approach which the players regard as being old-fashioned, patronising and arrogant when it is those very players that pull in the crowds.

All through this the players have repeatedly given their services for free to charities, most notably and recently to the naked calendar not to mention tonight's charity dinner for an ex-player now suffering from MS. All the players will be attending notwithstanding the current dispute.

Lawrence Dallaglio and captain Martin Johnson both agreed that they had taken this action regretfully and as a last resort but as former captain Matt Dawson pointed out the players have a short career, usually over by the time they are 34.

All we are asking for is a fair share of the substantial pot that these international games generate. We believe that this is a sentiment echoed by the clubs themselves who are still awaiting the resolution of a long-running dispute re their share of the revenue generated.

Whichever way you look at it, the players feel that the RFU is exhibiting a feudal attitude towards the players. In the words of Martin Johnson: 'It is sad that it has had to come to this but we made attempt after attempt to resolve this situation and have been met by nothing other than prevarication, excuses and general delaying tactics. It's only fair to everyone in the sport that this matter is addressed once and for all so we can all go forward and concentrate on the game.'

Lawrence Dallaglio confirmed that the players wish to resolve this quickly and amicably but made it clear that 'this decision was reached after a unanimous and secret ballot so there is no turning back now'.

Having left the hotel, Ben Cohen and I drove to my parents' house. Alastair Hignell's benefit dinner was that evening so it made sense for us to stay around London, and with all that had happened to Ben lately I was only too pleased to provide some company. We decided the best way to try to relax in the middle of all the chaos was to do some training at Farnham Rugby Club and we actually ended up doing a good session.

When we had finished, I found a message on my phone from Clive. It said that if I wasn't at training the next morning, the RFU's position was that my international career was at risk. That spelt out the situation pretty clearly. I didn't think there was much need to ring back immediately. Others had the same message. I spoke to two of the other coaches, Brian Ashton and Dave Alred, and they expressed the hope that they'd see us all again soon.

I didn't know what to think. One minute I would be reassuring myself it would all work out OK, the next I would find myself worrying that my England days were over at 21 and that I'd made the biggest mistake of my life.

Ben and I had a long drive into London to chew over the possibilities as we headed for the Café Royal that night. We met up with the rest of the squad there and compared messages. Those who had conducted the live phone chats held centre stage.

The RFU top brass were there, too, and Johnno was in and out of meetings with them all night. With Leicester's chief executive Peter Wheeler acting as a go-between, they had come up with a revised offer whereby the bonus we received if we won the Six Nations Championship was diverted into our match fees. It was a matter of £250 but we had moved their supposed final offer and raised our guaranteed pay level. We had not got what we wanted but then again, neither had the RFU. Compromise had been achieved. At a meeting at the end of the dinner, we decided to accept verbally. The strike was over 24 hours after it had begun. Johnno would meet the RFU next morning at Twickenham to sort out the final details.

The press were aware of the RFU's ultimatum but not of the peace deal and were out in force on Wednesday morning at Pennyhill Park to see if we would turn up. Ben had stayed with me at my parents' house so after receiving final clearance from Matt on the phone, we drove back to the hotel. We were first there and were besieged as we stepped out of the car. A scrum of journalists was waiting. There were cameras in our faces and questions being fired at us. Doing the decent thing, I pushed my way through and left Ben to face the music.

When we had made it to the hotel we took sanctuary in the physio's room and turned on the television. On Sky, there were pictures of the two of us arriving at Pennyhill Park. It looked like we were scabs. There was a worrying 10 minutes while we waited for the others to turn up but one by one they eventually did and the headline thankfully changed from 'Wilkinson and Cohen arrive back at hotel' to 'England team arrive back at hotel'. The whirlwind strike was over. All the England players were desperately relieved. We never wanted to miss the Argentina game, or any game for that matter.

People will think we were being greedy but we weren't asking for anything unreasonable. The money certainly wasn't going to set us up for life. All we wanted was some recognition that it was our efforts that helped to fill Twickenham and win big television contracts. We had gone through a lot together as a team and whether we won or not, we had never let each other or the country down. The idea behind striking was that we would never have to do so again. A long-term agreement was the goal.

The RFU honoured the verbal deal over match payments and bonuses but a formal contract remained unsigned. The issue was allowed to drift again as several matters, most importantly the business of intellectual property rights, remained unresolved. That was at the back of most players' minds when we were asked later on in the season by our clubs to support them in their long-running dispute with the Union. The clubs asked us to sign long-term contracts handing over our intellectual property rights to them.

Throughout their interminable negotiations, the players had largely stood back from it all. Wisely, given that we have a job to do, we had been left on the outside as the two sides talked. But as the major assets of the professional game, we do have an influence, and coming down on the side of the clubs was designed to bring a lasting agreement closer. It was a strong move meant to break the logjam in negotiations and bring a solution once and for all. We chose to support the clubs because we felt it was unfair that owners, including Dave Thompson at Newcastle, were having to pay our wages out of their pockets because they had not been given what they were owed by the RFU. With no agreement in place, there was no funding going from Twickenham to the clubs and as a player it wasn't a pleasant feeling knowing you were taking money straight out of club owners' pockets.

The Newcastle players were summoned to a meeting at which Rob Andrew outlined what we were being asked to do. We asked questions, satisfied ourselves of the details and decided to a man to sign the contracts.

A lot was made of the clause on player release for internationals. It required the clubs to give their prior permission, which some people interpreted as a potential problem. However, I don't think for one second any club would ever block their players turning out for England. From a personal standpoint, I know Rob well and I'm sure he would never want to have to stand in my way. He has played international rugby and knows that the feeling of playing at the highest level is one of the reasons we all work so hard for our clubs. The release clause ceased to be an issue when peace eventually broke out over the summer with an overdue long-term agreement between the clubs and the RFU which points to a rosy future for English rugby. I'm not saying our actions brought this about but I do think they helped bring people to the negotiating table.

Backing the clubs in this way caused a stir but it was a minor ripple compared with the shockwaves created by the strike. When people ask me if I would be willing to go through it all again, I am forced to say yes. Sometimes you have to make a stand.

I was pleased with the way the squad stayed together despite the efforts to break the strike. We were never arrogant or silly; we just stuck it out and believed in what we were doing.

There were some emotional difficulties from the whole business with some pretty forthright exchanges between the RFU and the players when we returned. It was probably best to get the anger and hurt out of everyone's system so that it did not fester. You only have to see Clive during England matches to understand that he can get as hyped up as the players – and it only takes a try to let you see this. He is intense throughout any international week and especially so on matchday when he often takes to the golf course to help mentally prepare himself for the game. What you see is what you get with Clive – he is extremely passionate about English rugby.

Ever since he took over he has done things his own way. He picked a young side and stuck with us even when he was under pressure and it takes a certain type of character with plenty of guts to do that. He wants his sides to go out to try to win rather than to avoid losing, which reflects his own personality and the way he used to play. Although he heads up the management team, he does not involve himself in every bit of hands-on coaching all that often, preferring sometimes to oversee the excellent team he has assembled.

It is very much an inclusive style of management with everyone asked to contribute, and Clive is very approachable. Johnno, Lawrence, Matt Dawson, Neil Back, Mike Catt and I speak to him regularly on tactics and preparation.

We were back training on Wednesday afternoon and with a day's lost work to catch up on, it was straight down to business. Almost inevitably, we had a great session back with the coaches.

After all the upheaval, the main interest around the game was what sort of reception we would be given by the Twickenham crowd. We need not have worried. There was a big group of supporters to meet us when we got off the bus and they gave us a huge cheer. It was the day Jason Leonard broke Rory Underwood's record for England caps and he led the side out so that guaranteed a favourable reception.

The game was a slight let-down. I'm convinced that the strike did not affect the performance in any way but the skies opened and made handling a real challenge. I opened the curtains on Saturday morning to leaden skies and the pitter patter of raindrops and my heart sank. Territory and possession were going to be massively important and once again our pack did a great job against the renowned Argentinian forwards with Mark Regan throwing in well on his recall.

In the wake of Kyran's blunder early in the week, Austin had tried to change the code words for backs' moves so they all became digs at him but we didn't have much chance to use them in the conditions. We did make some breaks but every time we opened up their defence, something seemed to go wrong. Iain Balshaw, picked ahead of Matt Perry at full-back after his storming performance as a sub against Australia, just missed one overlap and Lawrence Dallaglio lost his grip on the ball at the death with the line beckoning. It was that sort of day.

We did score one try, and the way it came about was similar to what had happened against Australia. The Pumas were a man short after a sin-binning and playing without a full-back, so we went for the chip through again. This time it was me doing the kicking and I threaded it through the defence, on to the post and Ben Cohen steamed up to score 12 minutes from time. It was a nice moment for him, after all he had been through, and from his celebration you could see he was pleased.

At the final whistle the main feeling was one of relief. We had put a difficult week behind us and beaten the Argentinians 19–0 in trying conditions. We had dealt with a decent side in a professional manner.

We were pleased to shut them out – that's a rare feat in international rugby – although Gonzalo Quesada, the 1999 World Cup's highest scorer, did us an unexpected favour by missing three penalties in the opening quarter of an hour.

If we had finished off a few more chances and scored more tries, the reaction might have been different but as it was we attracted a fair amount of criticism. I watched the television news after the game and they interviewed a couple of unimpressed spectators who thought we had played poorly. Everyone is entitled to their opinion but being criticised for effort really grates after all that you put in before the match and on the pitch.

I glanced at a couple of the papers later and they weren't particularly positive either. Some of the stick was directed at me. Mick Cleary, in the *Telegraph*, wrote:

> For the second week running, the England fly-half spluttered. He and Mike Catt alongside never found any rhythm or fluency in their partnership. Wilkinson is stuttering when he tries to find an inch or two of space. His speed is in his hands, not his legs, and he needs to work off those around him. His tactical kicking was also off-key.

Nobody likes to read that sort of thing about himself and normally I don't take much notice of it – the important thing is how the management, my family and my fellow players are reacting. While I was a little disappointed with the way I had played against Australia and Argentina – there were things I should have done differently – I was more than willing to swap a rave review for a victory. I agree we should have moved the ball more on certain occasions against the Pumas but we were trying to move towards winning big games and during the autumn we did that. We must have been doing something right.

Coming hot on the heels of the summer tour to South Africa where I seemed to attract a lot of praise, any perceived dip in form was frustrating but the nature of the game was different in England because of the wet conditions and the boggy pitches. I don't deny that in an ideal world I would choose to play a running game on fast, hard, dry pitches like the South African ones all the time. This was the first time I had played in an autumn series in England and the weather had been a huge factor.

At Newcastle I'm lucky because we have a surface that drains fantastically well but Twickenham, like other big stadia, was finding it harder to cope with deluges. The RFU had ordered a huge pitch cover but it wasn't going to be ready before the Six Nations so we just had to put up with quite heavy ground. That meant playing more of a kicking game, a different style from the one to which the English public have become accustomed. People can't have it both ways. Remember the flak when we lost to Scotland the previous season for trying to play too much rugby in a monsoon? We learnt from that experience and closed out Argentina with a more balanced game.

We knew we could play better but we had now won three consecutive matches against high-quality southern-hemisphere opposition and in the most pressurised circumstances. The next task was to make it four the following week.

chapter five

Sledging and the Springboks

For the duration of the autumn internationals I shared a room with Dan Luger. We moved out of the first room we were given because the shower wasn't working properly. That proved to be terrific luck because we were allocated a spectacular suite set on two floors, complete with its own putting machine. This was luxury – golf in your living room. We would take it in turns to design ever more complex courses, starting from obscure tee-off points behind the television and involving hazards such as Dan's jumper.

I'm not too bad at golf – I usually shoot somewhere in the mid 80s – but Dan doesn't play so I held the edge in these gripping contests. Controversy was never far away. Luger's ground-breaking 'back of the putter' stroke, which took him over the obstacles rather than around them, had to be outlawed.

Some of the lads prefer their own room when space allows but I enjoy a bit of company. Dan and I hit it off pretty well although not as well as the maids, who kept pushing our single beds together, seemed to think.

There are downsides to sharing a confined space and one of them is sharing germs. I had been suffering from a cold at the time of the Argentina game which I duly passed on to Dan ahead of the South Africa game the following week.

The snivelling and sneezing must have had something to do with the appalling weather. The rain was so bad that the hotel's pitch had become extremely heavy and we were forced indoors on Monday for some non-rugby drills, which made a change. There was five-a-side football, and a particularly ugly game of basketball preceded by a game that involved throwing tennis balls at an inflatable beach ball to try to propel it across the sports hall over a goal-line at the other end. It was backs against forwards, which was guaranteed to engender some bitter rivalry.

I was trying my hardest to hit the inflatable and win the game when it suddenly dawned on me that a lot of balls were flying a long way off target. We were under attack. Phil Greening seemed to be one of the main culprits so I launched one at his bald noggin and went perilously close to a bullseye. I thought I was the funniest guy in the world until Greening threw one back and it copped me right in the ear.

Greening is a gag merchant. On his answerphone message on his mobile, he shouts 'hello, hello' as if it's a bad line and he can't hear you properly. Then comes the punchline – 'only joking. Please leave your name and number . . .'

After that, we headed off to the training ground at Sandhurst, which was in better condition than the sodden hotel pitch, and preparations began in earnest. We knew South Africa would represent a very similar threat to the one Australia had posed. The Boks tend to go for the big hit more often though, which can occasionally leave holes if they mis-time the tackle. It can certainly sting if they don't.

One man we were acutely aware of was South Africa's full-back Percy Montgomery. He had hurt us in the World Cup quarter-final with his phenomenal kicking in open play, and he was also a dangerous counter-attacker. We knew our punting had to be very precise and our chasing good, too. We could not afford to give him time and space to set us back on our heels. This was an aspect I was going to have to work on particularly hard. However, when the Springboks named their side on Tuesday, Montgomery was at fly-half and Stefan Terblanche was at full-back. There were plenty of raised eyebrows.

True, Montgomery had recently played at fly-half against Argentina when they had experimented with more of a running game, but no one, including Clive, expected him to do so against England. Clive didn't believe Harry Viljoen's team selection, even though the Boks had put out a detailed description of Terblanche's past history at full-back in provincial rugby with their team announcement.

Sure enough, the South Africans released the real side two days later with Montgomery at full-back. Some pundits thought Viljoen was being underhand but I could understand his reasoning entirely. He wanted to throw us off our guard and disrupt our tactical preparations. It was just that we didn't fall for this trap.

Our side – the genuine one – had Matt Perry and Phil Greening return. Mike Catt had taken a bang in the ribs against Argentina and was struggling, so although he was named in the team we trained with Will Greenwood at inside-centre instead.

A lot of the talk at the press conference was related to the strike but the media were also interested in our selection at scrum-half where Matt Dawson had won his perennial battle with Kyran Bracken. That meant he would be going head to head with Joost van der Westhuizen, the man whom he dummied on the way to scoring that great try for the Lions in Cape Town in 1997. Playing outside Matt or Kyran makes little difference to me – their passes are quite similar. I'm just thankful we have two scrum-halves on a par with the best in the world.

The Tuesday session with the press is the only one that all the players attend prior to a weekend match. It serves a useful purpose in getting all the talking out of the way and it causes the adrenaline to flow by underlining the level of interest there is in the game. There are often 30 journalists, radio men and camera crews around the hotel. For me, as the bloke who sometimes puts over the kicks, it can be quite a busy couple of hours. At first I thought it was very flattering that lots of people wanted to speak to me but now I'm quite jealous of some of the others who don't have so much to do. What with television, radio, newspapers and the Internet to service, it can be quite hard work.

Richard Prescott, the RFU's communications director, briefs us beforehand on questions the media might ask but we still have to be on our toes. We have a policy that nobody says anything about the opposition which could be used as motivation.

I also provide a matchday column for the *Express*, which involves a chat with one of their journalists. He writes up the piece and sends it back to me. I generally show it to my dad – which involved faxing it to Australia before the South Africa game – and we double-check it before the final version goes into print. I'm extremely careful what I say. I want to put across the team's message.

We didn't overdo our own planning ahead of the match. We are encouraged to get our heads up, see what is happening on the pitch and react accordingly. There is a lot of trust given over to the players. We knew a fair amount about South Africa anyway from recent experience after sharing the summer series.

We had come so close in Pretoria, denied by that controversial call by the video referee. I missed the game because of a serious dose of food poisoning. A beef curry-type thing was to blame. It reappeared a few hours after I had eaten it and blocked a couple of sinks. Unfortunately, its legacy was the best part of a week spent in bed and the loss of half a stone. When I was eventually able to train again, my kicking was quite poor. Whether it was the altitude in Johannesburg where we were staying, the illness, or the type of ball we were using I'm not sure but things did not feel right. I was worried because it was crucial we levelled the series in the second Test in Bloemfontein. In terms of our development as a side, we just had to lay down a marker against one of the big three. I had no choice but to take a deep breath and put my trust in all the work I had done before – after all I had been kicking for 12 years. In the end, everything went like clockwork. We won 27–22 and I knocked over eight penalties and a drop goal. People were kind enough to say it had been my best performance for England, which was ironic given the erratic build-up. I had a chance in the last minute to equal the world record of nine penalties in a match but I put the ball into touch instead to make sure the final whistle blew.

The team's performance was fantastic – for some reason everyone seemed to be on exactly the right wavelength. Wherever I went, I knew my team-mates would be there for me and that made my job so much easier.

Victory provided an overwhelming sense of relief for the squad and a party was organised back at our Johannesburg base to celebrate. However, while we were up in the air, the fog descended on the High Veldt. The pilot tried to land once but was forced to pull out because of the conditions. It looked like we would have no option but to turn around, go back and spend a night in Bloemfontein, which would have been an anti-climax. The pilot must have felt the vibes from a frustrated England team because he went for it through the fog and landed perfectly.

I eventually got to bed about 4 a.m. after a great night at a club called Bourbon Street. The fact that the whole team, including the management, went out together summed up the spirit in the side. It was our end of season party.

Those thoughts were still relatively fresh in our minds and, having beaten the Boks in their own backyard, we were confident of being able to do it again at Twickenham. But South Africa seemed to have rediscovered the winning habit with victories against Argentina, Ireland

and Wales, the last two coming right at the death. What had struck me about the Boks was their patience. They had kept their composure as the games went down to the wire, and taken the crucial chances when they came about.

The Springboks were in a transitional phase under their new coach but the tremendous rugby tradition and the massive interest in the game meant their players were still under huge pressure to deliver results. That desperation and determination to succeed for their country is what has kept them at the top of the world game.

I didn't kick particularly well in training ahead of the game, particularly on Saturday morning. I kept trying and trying to get it right and in the end spent well over an hour working at it when I might have been better off with my feet up.

Am I too much of a perfectionist? That's a tricky one. Perfection is unattainable – I know that – but if you pay enough attention to something it will always have an effect. It is not easy for me to shrug my shoulders and walk away. I try to control what's controllable and not leave too much to chance. My boots, adidas Predators, are specially made for me. They follow the curves of my feet like slippers and have an extra layer of rubber placed across the tongue where I punt the ball for a better contact. The manufacturers want to put 'Wilko' on the tongues as well, at some stage in the future. Matt Dawson already has 'Daw' on his right boot and 'son' on the left. I wear each pair of boots until they become too soft but I always make sure I have a couple of spares with me for warm-up plus one other pair with different soles in case the ground conditions alter. I had my long studs packed for the heavy going against South Africa.

By the time the bus left the hotel for the ground at 11.50 I was still wound up from my frustrating morning. The extra shots at goal had taken 20 minutes, which doesn't sound much but that is the time when I like to relax before a match. I set an hour and a half aside for chilling out usually.

Hearing the Twickenham crowd singing 'Swing Low' before my first kick was inspiring, though, and somehow everything fell into place at the ground. I finished with a 100 per cent record, which contributed towards our 25–17 victory. It was great to get off to a good start but my most important kicks came in the second half. They were the ones that pushed our lead out to eight points and gave us a two-score cushion. Ever since the grand slam defeat against Wales at Wembley two seasons before, we had underlined the importance of closing a game out from a position of strength. We did that against South Africa by keeping them out of range.

Things went a lot better for me than in the previous two games in every area. I made quite a bit of ground with a jinking run early on but even more pleasing was Will Greenwood's try, which I had a hand in. Mike Catt was not fit, and on his comeback Will produced a lovely piece of deceptive running to score from a set move. It was my job to delay the pass to him to confuse the Springbok defence, and it went perfectly.

That was a moment of beauty in a fierce contest. A lot of blood was spilt but I didn't think it was a dirty game – in fact, I thought it was a good one. Rugby has always been an aggressive contact sport.

The South Africans were hyped up – of that there is no doubt – but not overly so. Both teams set out to intimidate each other. We took a few shots but so did they, and we all shook hands afterwards. The South African captain, Andre Vos, made a point of asking after my health at the end. I was cut in the first couple of minutes by a flying wrist to the head as I was tackled. I should really have had it stitched but there was no time for that so I had it taped up. I never got around to being stitched afterwards either so I have a little scar as a reminder of our victory. It's better than a tattoo.

My cut was just a nick compared with the gashes suffered by Richard Hill and Neil Back, which needed 31 stitches. Phil Greening had his finger broken but all three returned to the field. It was typical of the commitment we showed.

It looked for all the world as though South Africa had scored an early try when Montgomery stepped his way through our defence, but Richard Hill somehow managed to get his body under the ball over the line. While we were waiting to restart play, there was a fairly ferocious bout of sledging from Robbie Fleck aimed at Mike Tindall. Fleck had got himself yellow carded in Cardiff the previous week against Wales and he was clearly up for this game as well. Mike gave him plenty of verbals back and we got on with the match.

Sledging is part of the game these days. I take plenty of it and I know who to expect it from. Greening and Andy Gomarsall cough 'miss' at me in club matches as I'm preparing a goalkick. I don't mind – it adds to the enjoyment as far as I'm concerned. I might even say a few words if I'm pumped up after a big tackle, but usually I'm more concerned with talking to my team-mates. Although it goes against my nature, I try to be noisy on the pitch – there's no use being a shrinking violet if you are trying to organise things.

For some people, the verbal side is more important than it is for others. Austin Healey, for instance, does a lot of talking. He came up behind me and sneered 'good afternoon, Wilko' annoyingly during the Leicester game at Kingston Park. That was one of his more printable remarks, anyway.

Mike Catt is another one. If you do something well he is magnanimous enough to offer his congratulations. I find myself saying 'nice kick' sometimes to opponents. It doesn't mean I won't be trying any harder to flatten them next time around.

The victory against South Africa was a professional job well done and the end of the autumn series. Despite the turmoil, it had been a highly successful three weeks and we concluded it with a night on the town. We went to the Sugar Reef bar in the West End and then on to a nightclub called Cafe Paris. They are getting to know us at Sugar Reef, as we've been before and can almost guarantee to get in. There's no superstar syndrome though – we still queue at the bar like everyone else.

Lawrence Dallaglio is probably the best-known player in English rugby, for various reasons, and trying to keep up with his ferocious walking pace was a real eye-opener. Every few yards a taxi driver, tourist or reveller would recognise him and give him a shout. He must feel like he is living in a goldfish bowl. He handles it really well but the enormous pressure of being public property must lead to a bizarre existence. The night ended with me playing the piano in the early hours in the hotel reception. Asked politely to go to bed by the staff, I obliged. I can't play the piano.

It was a bit of a one-off the whole squad going out together. After home Six Nations games there is a formal dinner at the Hilton Hotel and, with families coming along, different groups split off. I tend to go out with Phil Greening, Danny Grewcock or Richard Hill. This time we were pretty much out as a team and we made the most of it.

As some hangovers faded next day, we were left to reflect on what we had achieved and where we were heading. We had beaten three southern-hemisphere sides in consecutive weeks, which was quite a record. Developing the winning habit against these sides was a big plus. It helped to remove the mystique surrounding them. No one could doubt our commitment and our organisation in doing this but we had to concede we hadn't completely set the world alight with our attacking play. The heavy ground had not helped but as a side we had been frustrated by our lack of tries. Three in three games was under-par.

The thought crossed my mind that if we could combine some of the running rugby we had produced in the previous season's Six Nations with the ability to win big games that we had developed during the autumn, we could become quite a side.

Unfortunately, we would have to wait two months until we took on Wales in Cardiff to find out if that was possible.

chapter six

Descent into madness

A familiar face was missing when I returned to Newcastle. John Leslie had left for Northampton. The exact truth of how and why he had gone was difficult to assess but the basic reason was that Rob Andrew did not think he was going to be playing consistent first team rugby. He wanted Tom May and Jamie Noon to play and grow as the club's centre partnership.

JL arrived at Newcastle from Japan as a world-beater, having been the player of the Five Nations Championship in 1999. He had exceptional talent and was a great bloke with it, but the ankle injury he sustained in the World Cup continued to cause problems and he was never able to be quite the force he knew he could be under different circumstances.

He played a few games at the end of the 1999–2000 season when it was obvious he wasn't physically right. He must have been desperate to play to show his new colleagues what he could do. In the end, he had to undergo a second operation in the summer. After he proved his fitness in pre-season, a lot was expected of the pair of us as a midfield combination. We didn't click immediately, although I very much enjoyed playing with him. I have to shoulder some of the blame for things turning out badly for JL. It takes a while for any pairing to get to know each other's game but the problem here was that we didn't have time on our side. In every game something a little different would crop up.

There were difficulties over when he wanted the ball quickly to take on his man and when he wanted the timing changed to allow him to draw opponents in and then get the pass away. Team-mates had the occasional trouble reading him. His special abilities enabled him to find holes in defences when others wouldn't, but when he threw a pass some players weren't there quickly enough to receive it. When it worked – and sometimes it did – it was outstanding.

After JL had been substituted a few times, Newcastle played Tom May for a while. They obviously wanted to explore their options. Professional rugby union is a cut-throat business and everyone in it is aware of how harsh it can be. JL hardly had time to unpack his boxes in his new home near mine before he had to pack them again.

Nevertheless, it came as a bolt out of the blue to be told by my brother the news that JL was leaving. I was with England at the time. But even in my brief career I have seen a pretty big turnover of players and all I could do was get on with my own game. I knew the partnership with Tom had worked in the past and I was confident it would again in the future. However, JL is hilarious, and a superb guy to have around. I am glad he is still playing in the Premiership and look forward to seeing him again.

Going back to club rugby after the emotion of playing for England is not as difficult as people make out. The crowds and the attention are a lot smaller but if that's all you're playing rugby for, maybe you need to re-examine your priorities. My main aim is to win and it doesn't matter whether I'm at Kingston Park or Twickenham.

I'm nervous before Premiership matches as well as internationals and the reason is the importance I place on myself performing to the same level in both. I want to be able to look my team-mates in the eye afterwards and tell them I gave it everything. It is their respect I crave, not anyone's on the outside.

My ambition is to become the best fly-half in the world and every match helps me move towards that goal. I learn a lot from Test rugby, sure, but I take something from every Premiership game. Where the two differ very slightly is in terms of mental fatigue. It takes a while to sort your head out after Test matches and with this in mind Newcastle left me out of the side for the league match at London Irish three days after the Springbok match.

I would have had no qualms about playing if I had been asked but a spell on the sidelines was probably a good idea, particularly the way Dave Walder had been playing in my absence. 'Walnut' is my training partner. He has a similar work ethic to me and we often practise goalkicking together. He doesn't need to do all that much work because he has so much natural ability in striking a ball, but occasionally I help with some fine-tuning. All those hours of practice mean I know the mechanics of goalkicking pretty well by now.

Dave scored all 32 points in the victory over Saracens, a fact Kyran Bracken reported back with unhealthy emphasis in the England camp. I was obviously pleased but the timing could have been better after the criticism of my performance against Argentina. I didn't fancy being dropped by club and country.

While beating Sarries was a great win, the boys had lost at Northampton so it was important to pick up some more points at Irish. Finding myself in a spectator's role for the game was unusual. Normally I'm a terrible watcher. This time I tried to detach myself as best I could. I stayed out of the changing room before kick-off and sat in the stand.

Irish were in their first season at the Madejski Stadium and the jury was still out over whether their decision to move out of London to Reading was working. The place looked empty until just before kick-off. Then the bars and car parks emptied and suddenly there was a great atmosphere. The ground lends itself to excitement. The view is terrific for spectators, the surface is good for players and it feels like somewhere special. Irish had done a good job in making the Madejski their home. Unfortunately, that also extended to winning regularly there and we went down 19–17. We threw the game away really, but one positive thing was that we were not travelling back until the next day. It was an evening kick-off so we wouldn't have reached Newcastle until 5 a.m.

When we did return there was a pleasant distraction in the form of a touch rugby 10s tournament at the Royal Grammar School, Newcastle. Every Falcons player is allocated a particular school for the season as part of the club's work in the community, and this was mine. I was asked to take a Newcastle team along to play against the school's first team, the old boys and the staff. It is so rare now for professional players to take part in rugby with a party atmosphere that this came as a welcome release. We took a tasty side along. It included some great broken-field players in Michael Stephenson, Dave Walder and Andrew Mower, and gave me a chance to play with my brother – something I'd like to do more of.

It was like being transported back to my own schooldays. The changing room had that familiar smell and contained the inevitable lost property bucket with an assortment of forgotten gear. My brother picked out an amazing pair of pre-war boots, one of which had a single stud nailed into the centre. He wore them for a warm-up routine that had us in stitches, but sadly took them off for the matches. The Falcons avoided embarrassment by coming out on top and, with the pupils crowding the touchline, scored some entertaining tries.

My off-field duties extended to posing for some pictures for a coaching column in the *Express*. Nivea were backing a strip cartoon in the paper every Saturday, teaching youngsters the basics of rugby. My dad and I came up with the words to run alongside a series of pictures of me carrying out various skills, ranging from punting to tackling. I needed a stooge for the pictures to make me look good and Hall Charlton, Newcastle's reserve scrum-half, took on the role. He suffered badly, having to be side-stepped, knocked over and generally made to look a fool. Allen Chilten, the other reserve, was another victim. But the biggest star of the show was Ray the cap-wearing groundsman, who featured probably more than me.

The Nivea link-up also entailed a photo-shoot that involved me being plastered in mud. The photographer brought along a cosmetic version but the pitch was pretty boggy at the time so, in the end, I just scooped a couple of handfuls off the ground and used that instead. Rugby players do not make very good pampered supermodels.

Back at the office, our next Premiership appointment was at the Memorial Ground, Bristol on 16 December. On long trips like this some light relief is always welcome. I was rooming with Gary Armstrong for this one and late in the evening the phone rang. Gary answered it. He listened for a while but became increasingly irritated and ended up putting the phone down on the caller. 'What was that about?' I asked. He explained that someone calling himself Mohammed, and claiming to be from Jedforest, wanted to have breakfast with him at the hotel in the morning. He claimed to be a big fan of his, but Gary smelled a rat. He couldn't remember many Asians at borders rugby matches and thought it must be a wind-up.

Shortly afterwards, an angry Mohammed rang back, claiming to have been insulted by the phone being put down on him. I took the call and tried to catch out whichever team-mate of ours it was with some in-depth interrogation. He was good, though, and after a few questions I panicked and handed him over. Gary put the phone down on him again. When he called a third time, livid at his treatment, Gary just burst out laughing and cut him off once more. We never did find out who he was; so Mohammed, if you happen to be real, sorry for being so rude.

The game the next day was a big disappointment. We made enough opportunities to have won the game but wasted them. In contrast, when Bristol scented the try-line they finished aggressively. We won plenty of ball late on but left ourselves too much to do and went down 27–14. The game marked the beginning of a mini-crisis for me with my goalkicking. I kicked two out of four but even one of the successes was a mis-hit.

I worked like a madman on the training ground before the trip to Gloucester the following week. I didn't see much of home in that period. In fact, I was so preoccupied I hardly realised Christmas was coming. It was frustrating not being able to rely on an aspect of my game that is usually fairly good, and the only way to sort it was on the training ground.

I kicked after the team run during the day and then came back at night on my own. Dave Walder was struggling with a groin injury so I had no choice. Sometimes I worked with my brother but he had his job to do with the Under-21s and although I knew he would uncomplainingly fetch balls for me all night, I didn't think it was fair to ask him. I can honestly say I was never lonely – I was too absorbed in what I was doing.

The wind that howls around Kingston Park seemed to ease at night. It had been particularly strong of late which made practising difficult. To minimise the disruption, I tried to kick into the wind – that way it does not affect the ball's flight too much. All it does is make the distance the ball travels shorter. As darkness fell, I would load a bag full of balls into the boot of my car, drive to Kingston Park, and Ray the groundsman would put the floodlights on. My lapses were eating away at me and I was becoming a desperate case as one particular kicking session proved.

The way I train is to divide my kicking into sets of five. After practising for a while, if I'm happy with the final set, I'll go home. This time, for some reason, the record got stuck. Whatever I did, one of the five went astray. I just could not satisfy myself. What I had promised myself would be my last set ended up taking an hour and a quarter. I'm just glad a psychiatrist wasn't watching. The whole session lasted two and a half hours.

Dave Alred came up to Newcastle to help with some technical aspects but I headed down to Gloucester for our next game with my confidence still low. I wanted to be out kicking all the time to sort out the gremlins, but the long journey down to Kingsholm meant a day without a kick. I was like a junkie without my fix.

Gloucester started the game superbly. We made a couple of defensive errors and suddenly they were two tries to the good. The match was already beyond us and they stretched away after the break to a 28–6 lead before we finally got our act together and played with a lot more energy and purpose. The reward was a consolation try, which I scored at the death. I had managed a couple of breaks and this time I was able to go all the way on the outside and touch down. I was tackled short of the line but sensed it was close and stretched out to score, taking a whack in the ribs for my trouble as I did so. Some of the Gloucester lads weren't too happy with the decision but the ball was on the line, which counts as a try. I put over the conversion to finish with three out of five but things still weren't right with my kicking. I had to sort out the glitches for my own sanity.

On Christmas Eve, Mark and I went to Kingston Park and that hour and a half's toil finally helped me to turn the corner. Frost was forecast so the pitch was supposed to be covered to protect it but we persuaded our groundsman Ray to leave one end open and I set to work. I stripped down my kicking technique to make sure everything was OK with the component parts, and then built it up again. The session went really well and we went home in a positive frame of mind.

Our parents had come up for Christmas and we planned to spend the day with my aunt in Great Ayton. However, I wanted to make sure I hadn't lost any of the momentum I had gained the day before, so I nipped out early on Christmas morning for half an hour's kicking. Some people might regard this as certifiable behaviour but that's the way I have always been and I suspect always will be. It worked, and I was able to put it all to one side, relax and enjoy a traditional Christmas with my loved ones.

The festive season isn't the best time of year to be a rugby player but the way the fixture list worked out with a home game against Bristol on 27 December meant I had more of a normal holiday period than usual. The previous season, Newcastle played away at Northampton on Boxing Day so we spent Christmas evening on a bus, travelling down for the game. It was actually quite enjoyable because everyone was in a good mood after family celebrations earlier on.

This year Santa Claus brought me a trouser press which was very nice except it couldn't do shirts as well. I like clothes and do a bit of shopping in Newcastle but I don't seem to have the occasion to wear much of my gear except the training kit.

Being fortunate enough to earn a good salary means I don't really want for anything but I'm not extravagant. I do have a pool table and when I get round to it I'm going to have a gym room at home. CDs are also a minor indulgence, cutting across a wide range of tastes – everything from the Beatles to old school rap, Al Green to Travis.

My brother and I bought Dad a digital camera and Mum a cashmere pashmena, which was a bit of a gamble on my part – I kept the receipt – but it seemed to be a winner.

Christmas dinner was a fill your face affair. Usually I have to be careful what I eat but turkey and veg is a pretty healthy option. Overdoing the alcohol is a definite no-no but since I hardly drink, and never have wine anyway, I didn't miss out. The Wilkinson boys hosted the Boxing Day meal. I'd just like to stress the word 'hosted' – not 'cooked'. Mum came to the rescue on that score and was also games master. After running a treasure hunt the previous day, she came up with another one which involved us all hunting down place names hidden on scraps of paper around the house. I wasn't much of a competitor, half asleep after the mental stress and physical exertions of the previous couple of weeks, but judging by the shouting, which kept me awake, it was a success.

On Boxing Day we had a team training session to fit in ahead of the return league match against Bristol. The plunging temperatures had put the game in some doubt but covering Kingston Park worked, up to a point. Although the pitch was playable when the game started, it hardened up during the game and by the end, the players' boots sounded like horses' hooves, echoing on the unforgiving surface.

Kicking was extremely difficult and if ever a situation was guaranteed to expose any problems, this was the one. I wasn't confident of being able to keep my feet if I gave the ball a proper thump so I opted to try to control the kicks instead. It couldn't have gone better in terms of striking the ball. I would have finished with seven out of eight but for some innovative tactics from Bristol. They opted to hoist 6ft 6in Garath Archer up in front of the bar so as the ball dipped, he could catch it. He managed to block two. I think lifting a player to block a penalty should be outlawed. It isn't really fair to have a goalkeeper in rugby. If you cannot charge down a penalty, why should you be able to deflect it?

In the event, I was happy enough. We won, thanks to a great performance from Gary Armstrong, and my kicking was returning to something like its normal self. It was becoming second nature once again. Nevertheless, when the *Daily Mail* came out the next day, the headline read something along the lines of 'Super Armstong rescues wayward Wilkinson'. I was livid. I had worked so hard to get things right only to be slagged off in print. I try not to read the papers because of this sort of thing but I had overheard my mum telling our neighbours I'd had a poor write-up when we went round for a drink the following day. Foolishly I searched out the offending article and was infuriated when I read it.

I can accept criticism when it is deserved but this was simply misleading. The report said I had missed six kicks at goal. Three of those were drop kicks, which were pretty tricky in the conditions, given that I was in danger of copping one on the chin with the exaggerated bounce of the ball. Of the drop goal attempts, one was a 45-yarder I had gone for knowing we had already been awarded a penalty so it was a free hit, the others were tactical as much as anything to keep Bristol in their own territory. Despite this sour note, I felt cheered by my performance.

With our last match of 2000, against Harlequins, cancelled because of the weather, the Falcons ended the year in style. It had been an interesting and challenging couple of weeks.

New Year's Eve was a great day. One of my friends from the previous season's squad, Harley Crane, was staying and being a top host I cooked a special breakfast. Harley, Mark and I all wore jacket and tie to commemorate the occasion and they were suitably underwhelmed by my omelettes. Then it was cards at the breakfast table and off to Town Moor in Jesmond for a snowball shoot-out and some sledging. We didn't have a sledge so I used Mark and a plastic sheet and gave him a dead leg. Quite a few of the Newcastle boys were there but there was no Doddie. He had a good excuse. Just after Christmas little Hamish had arrived – he had become a father.

After a few drinks down on the Quayside where there were to be fireworks and a street party, we went on to Tom May's and had a great night. He had shrewdly taken the precaution of stripping the flat bare of furniture.

A year that had started with frowns ended all smiles and, I'm pleased to say, with my mental health intact.

chapter seven

Pastures new

England's trip to Wales had been occupying minds and making mouths water for months. Whatever we had managed to achieve during the autumn, this was a daunting prospect. In many respects it was the ideal game for the first weekend of the Six Nations Championship.

As usual, England started as tournament favourites but our first trip to the Millennium Stadium was being billed as an appointment in the lion's den, and with good reason. Wales were an ever-improving side. In Scott Quinnell, Rob Howley and Scott Gibbs they had world-class players in key positions, backed up by plenty of enthusiasm to win.

Quinnell had attracted some criticism over his fitness the previous season but we perceived Scott as a real strength rather than any kind of weakness. He would be a handful. Howley was at the top of his game, a real menace if he was allowed an inch of room, and everyone knew what Gibbs, who was winning his 50th cap, was capable of.

The Welsh clubs had gone well in the Heineken Cup up until the previous weekend when Leicester and Gloucester had beaten Swansea and Cardiff respectively. This was being portrayed in the media as a psychological advantage to us but a big club game is one thing, Six Nations rugby is quite another.

The standard of the club game has risen so much in recent years that the gap between the two in terms of quality is getting ever smaller. What is different is the extra something that the international stage brings out in players. It is impossible for the Premiership or the Welsh-Scottish League to replicate the hype and the crowds that follow the international game. Performing somewhere like the Millennium Stadium under a huge pressure of expectation inevitably demands a little bit extra from players.

The England squad had continued to meet up on Mondays, gearing ourselves up for this one game. There was no talk of grand slams or of titles, only of this match. It was massively important for us to get off to a good start in the tournament. Clive Woodward said a win in Cardiff would mean as much to him as anything we had achieved in the autumn.

It was the first time I had played an international in Wales. I was nervous but I couldn't wait. I love the passion the Welsh bring to their club rugby and I knew we were in for quite a reception in Cardiff. I wasn't disappointed.

We did most of our preparation for the game at our usual Pennyhill Park base before travelling to Wales on the Thursday, with the idea of minimising the disruption to our usual routine. The plan was to go in our own cars, which presented a problem or two for certain members of our squad. Phil Greening was turned back at the toll bridge because he didn't have any money and had to head back into Bristol to find a cash point. Apparently they didn't take his Visa.

Phil was recovering from a knee operation at the time and his place had gone to Dorian West but he had stayed with the squad, primarily to annoy us. He tried to niggle me by christening me Darius after a character I found quite loathsome in ITV's 'Popstars' programme, but fortunately it didn't stick.

Dorian was a good stand-in. Born in North Wales, he had made it clear where his allegiances lay these days, and he was playing some great rugby for Leicester. At 33 he was a latecomer to international rugby, having shadowed Richard Cockerill at Welford Road for a long time.

His inclusion meant more taxing work for the squad nickname boffins. Nobby was his usual pseudonym but he was initially referred to as 'The Chief' because of his habit of calling everyone 'chief'. That was harmless enough but when the Leicester boys let on that he had a reputation for spending time with the Tigers' manager Dean Richards, Mark Regan came up with Pila fish. This is a creature that hangs around the big fish out at sea.

It was all good, light-hearted stuff but behind the smiles I had a lot on my mind. My groin was playing up after I pulled it in training at Newcastle. The pain was on the same side as the operation but it wasn't a recurrence of that problem. I told our team doctor, Terry Crystal, and he passed on the information to the management. Clive checked with me whether I would be OK for the game and I said I would. I had to miss half a session in the build-up and undergo some ultra-sound treatment from the physiotherapists, but by Thursday it had improved markedly. I was in.

Clive had sprung a surprise or two in selection by bringing in Iain Balshaw to start at full-back and pairing Will Greenwood and Mike Catt in the centre. Since the autumn, the management had been poring over ways in which we might be more effective in turning possession into points. We felt there might be space out wide against Wales and Balsh's sprinter's pace was to be employed to exploit that. He adds a lot to the team.

It was tough on Matt Perry, though, especially as the two were team-mates at Bath where Balsh played on the wing. I felt for Matt because he hadn't put a foot wrong for England and had been through a lot for his country. He took it superbly and was extremely positive about the decision even though he must have been cut up inside.

Will Greenwood's inclusion was slightly different. Most people had judged it to be an either/or selection between Will and Mike Catt. Will plays most of his rugby at inside-centre, and was being asked to play outside-centre. However, the centres had been swapping positions during our Monday sessions and Will was quite happy to play there. He had been in great form since his summer move back to Harlequins from Leicester, and he had gone well against South Africa in Mike Catt's absence. This was seen as a way to involve him in the side. Mike Tindall, my old England Schoolboy friend and another guy to have played very well and done very little wrong, was the one to miss out.

We got together to work out how to get the best out of Will. He isn't exactly the same type of player as Mike – he goes in and out of tackles rather than through them – but he was quick to get to grips with the demands of his new role and I was very happy with the look of our midfield. We had trained well – now all we had to do was replicate that with Scott Gibbs and Mark Taylor flying up at us. Easier said than done!

Martin Johnson was there to lead us in Cardiff, which was a relief as he could have been suspended following an incident at Saracens way back in November. The case took so long to be examined that there was a real danger he would miss the Wales game. As it was, his five-week ban for a knee-drop on Duncan McRae expired just before the match. Martin is such a great player and an intimidating presence that he would have been sorely missed by England.

He took a lot of flak over the incident but he is not, by instinct, a dirty player. Rugby is a physical game and some of what goes on is right on the edge of the law. The odd unsavoury act will always occur. What players are trying to do with the odd shot is not to injure an opponent but to affect them psychologically. It is a mental battle as well as a physical one. While it is right to try to make the game as clean as possible, it would be wrong to sanitise it completely. Many of the best players have an intimidatory aura which helps their teams to win. Johnno is one of them.

A lot had been made of the Millennium Stadium in the build-up. On the day before the game we were given our first taste of the new home of Welsh rugby. There was a surprise awaiting us when we arrived at the ground – the Welsh team were in our dressing room, not the real deal but life-sized cardboard cut-outs of each player. Scott Quinnell was in my place. He looked pretty big. We were slightly bemused by this but we left them there unmolested. I don't know whether it was intended to psych us out – officials said they had been left there after a stadium tour – but if it was meant to affect us it didn't work. There were some life-sized inflatable Martin Johnsons outside the ground to provide back-up.

My first impression of the stadium was that it was a wonderful rugby ground, atmospheric even when it was empty. What it would be like packed with 70,000 Welshmen I didn't care to think about.

There had been a lot of controversy over the state of the pitch, particularly with football's Worthington Cup final just around the corner. It had been completely relaid ahead of our match and looked in immaculate condition, and that was clearly the way they wanted it to stay. I was there to practise my goalkicking ahead of the game, which is a courtesy extended by each country in the Six Nations. Unfortunately, nobody seemed to have briefed the groundstaff.

I always start my sessions by kicking off the turf, rather than a tee, and to stand the ball up I needed to make a mark with my boot. One of the groundstaff took exception to this and asked me not to do it. He offered me some sand to use instead but I didn't want it. Dave Alred, who was with me and can work a nice line in sarcasm, asked him what they planned to do if there was a five-metre scrum the next day – cancel the game? I didn't want a major diplomatic incident so I fobbed the guy off and, when he wasn't looking, knocked over a few more.

When I was happy, I moved on to the kicking tee but this didn't seem to satisfy the locals. Someone else came along and asked me to keep moving around so I didn't stand on the same spot and damage the pitch. I wonder if Neil Jenkins received this sort of earache?

When I finally got down to business without being pestered, I found the enclosed nature of the stadium helped the balls to travel further. The temperature seemed to be warmer inside than out. A rugby ball is no different from a squash ball – if it is heated up, it moves faster. That was one thing to bear in mind for matchday.

We returned to our hotel in Cardiff Bay and watched the Wales-England A team match on TV that evening. The Welsh language commentary proved a test but we could manage to understand the scoreline, which at the final whistle showed a draw. We expected our game to be just as competitive.

The hotel's location gave me a problem finding a usable patch of grass for kicking practice on the morning of the game. The only available option nearby seemed to be the playground of a primary school over the road. It was a bit of a bog but just about did the job, even though I did genuinely have to use jumpers for goalposts. There were cars driving past beeping their horns and kids hanging around, which made concentration a challenge, but I was quite happy with how it went. In fact, as a preamble to what would be a hostile environment at the ground, the cat-calling was perfect.

The bus journey to the ground was something else. As always, I sat by the window next to Ben Cohen with Austin Healey and Lawrence Dallaglio up at the front in charge of the music – dance, again. Nice. The Millennium Stadium stands right at the heart of the city and to reach it from the bay area meant running the gauntlet of packed narrow streets. As the bus edged through, we were roundly abused by the Welsh. The English fans we encountered gave us supportive gestures; their Welsh counterparts something different. It was quite an eye-opener and totally removed from anything I had experienced in Scotland, Ireland or Italy.

I was also thrown offguard when we arrived at the ground – some roses had been left in the dressing room for me by an apparent admirer.

There was little romance when we warmed up on the pitch. The video screens were showing the match at Wembley two years ago and Scott Gibbs's injury-time try. It was intended to stoke up the crowd, but seeing it again jarred. That defeat cost us a grand slam – it was personal. Just like at Wembley that day, Max Boyce was on the field, telling the crowd they could make the difference, and when we ran out, boy did they try. The noise was incredible. The boos were deafening and the crowd felt so close. When the Welsh team ran out, the place exploded. We knew we had to stick together.

The Welsh hit us with a whirlwind start. Mike Catt was hit hard by Scott Gibbs from the kick-off – he was taken out in the air so it could have been a penalty. That set the tone for five minutes of desperate defence but we survived. The video screen was called into play to rule on one possible try but Ben Cohen came to the rescue by winning the race to the touchdown. Then we lost Dan Luger with a neck injury, but the way we came through that early assault was vital – it was a show of strength.

Our response to the onslaught was immensely satisfying. We ran in six tries and any thoughts of a Wilkinson-Neil Jenkins penalty shoot-out never materialised. Will Greenwood's two tries within three minutes in the opening quarter turned the game our way and helped to defuse the crowd. Home advantage can be critical but the place went a little quiet then. Two more tries from Matt Dawson before the interval gave us a 29–8 lead. We went in on a high at half-time but Clive Woodward and the coaches immediately had to bring us back down. By the time the second half kicked off we had to be back at base camp mentally, ready to start the game afresh. Running through our usual routine helped stop heads spinning and ensured no complacency. Although we were frustrated with the way we finished the game, a final score of 44–15 was probably more than we could have asked for.

Mike Catt and Will Greenwood, who went on to score a hat-trick, fitted together superbly in the centre and Iain Balshaw came in and played with real pace. The magnificent surface, and dry weather, helped us to play attacking rugby. Our backs performed well but it was the phenomenal workrate of the forwards that laid the foundation for us. They were superb.

There were things to work on. We conceded turnovers, blew a couple of try-scoring opportunities and let Wales in for a couple of tries, but we had to be pleased with our start to the championship. Graham Henry, the Welsh coach, was extremely complimentary about our performance. He was, of course, the Lions coach as well, but at the time his dual role did not even enter my head. Impressing him came a long way behind doing the job for England.

Spirits were high in the England dressing room after the game. Prince William came in to talk to us and I had a word with him about his gap year, the game and his brother Harry, who is a big rugby fan. He spoke to most of the players and everything was very civilised until Austin, who had come on as a replacement for Dan Luger, emerged naked from the shower. He spotted his opportunity to end up locked in the Tower and revealed himself to the future king, shouting, 'Oi, Wills, do you want some of this?'

Calm as you like, William replied, 'If that's all you've got, Austin, I'm not going to bother.'

We fell about laughing and every time Austin opened his mouth that evening he was reminded of his royal humbling.

Amid the good humour, my mind turned to another, more sombre, event which had been going on that day. It was a memorial service for a boy called Neil Woods. I had met Neil, an 11-year-old with an incurable tumour, in September. He was a pupil at St Olave's School in York and a keen rugby player. Neil came up to Newcastle for a day and was the Falcons mascot when we played Wasps. He ran out on to the pitch with me before the game and afterwards I gave him my Newcastle shirt and a pair of boots I had worn in South Africa during the summer. A month later, Neil came back to Kingston Park to watch another game. He was in a wheelchair and it was a freezing, rainy day but he stuck it out nonetheless.

Neil died just before Christmas. At his funeral my Newcastle shirt was placed on his coffin. I would like to have been at his memorial service but the Wales game made that impossible. I sent a message. Since then I have always tried to get the Woods family tickets for Twickenham matches. Ian, Sylvia and Dominic, Neil's brother, are now close friends of the Wilkinsons.

At the reception, Neil Jenkins presented me with a Cardiff shirt with his name across the back. It was a return gesture because he had asked me for a Newcastle shirt earlier in the season. It was a really nice surprise and I was honoured.

Earlier there had been a less pleasant surprise. On our way to the dinner our bus was involved in an accident. There were a lot of people milling around, some of them I fear a little drunk, and one person was knocked down by the wing mirror. He was OK but we had to stop and wait for an ambulance. The mood outside was quite boorish and heated – one bloke head-butted the side of the bus, splitting his own head open – and the police arrived to keep people back. We were glad to get off the coach and into the dinner.

Dan's injury, which was to keep him out until the end of the season, meant he could not attend the dinner so a substitute was needed. I persuaded Phil Greening to go. He had to borrow Dan's dinner suit, which of course didn't fit, and wear it with his red snakeskin shoes. He didn't have a bow tie either. In that outfit he had little chance of repeating his bachelor successes of the autumn, but it didn't stop him trying.

During the dinner, a waiter passed a message across to me with a girl's name and number on it. 'Phone me' it said. I thought I had escaped without anyone else spotting the note but Iain Balshaw's eagle eyes picked it out. He pinched it and showed it to everyone, including Greening. Phil phoned the number, got through to an answer phone and left a message saying, 'Hi, it's Jonny. Please get back to me.' He left his own number at the end. It never came to anything for him, but he wasn't too bothered as soon after he met his new partner, Lucy.

I couldn't castigate Phil on the dinner-suit front. I hired mine but forgot to take it back afterwards and ran up a bill of £120. I bought one a fortnight later.

I stayed in the south for a couple of days, joining up with Liam Botham to attend a testimonial dinner for Rob Andrew and Tony Underwood, but then it was back to club business. Bath were the next up.

It had been snowing in the north east and the thaw had rendered Kingston Park unplayable so preparations were diverted to Middlesbrough Football Club's training complex. Apparently, there were semi-astroturf pitches waiting for us, as well as a showroom-full of Porsches in the car park.

It was the first time any of us had been there so we set off in convoy with maps only to find the police blocking the route we needed to take. The flooding had closed the road so a detour was required. Steve Bates was up at the front of the queue in the Falcons mini-bus, and from my car I could see him talking to the policeman. The directions he was being given seemed to be quite complex. It took a long time to explain them but eventually Steve drove off.

Tom May and Jamie Noon were in the next car. They pulled up and told the policeman they were heading for Middlesbrough's training pitch. He explained that the road was closed and told them to follow their mate. They claimed not to know Steve so the policeman had to go through the whole set of directions again for their benefit. Off they went.

Ian Peel was next. He had picked up on the joke and fed the policeman the same line. Patiently, he went through the whole rigmarole once more before driving off. We were next. I thought about it but I couldn't go through with it. I drove off after Ian and hoped I didn't lose him on the way.

After a week with England, preparing for the Bath game meant playing with different team-mates and running through different moves. It took a while to get used to.

In a way, the Bath match was a mini Test because of the number of international players involved. It was a great chance for our up-and-coming young backs, who were already beginning to attract some attention nationally, to make a mark on some of the established England players, and they took it. It was one of our best games of the season. Not only did we beat an in-form and very good side 24–23 but we played some great rugby in front of Kingston Park's biggest-ever crowd.

Dave Walder put me in for an early try; I returned the compliment for him just before half-time and when Gary Armstrong scored in the 54th minute we looked safe-ish at 24–13. But Bath came back superbly and we had to endure some jittery moments at the end before the final whistle.

The victory meant a lot and I would have loved to reflect on it with my team-mates but there was barely time for a lap of honour before heading off to Teesside Airport to rejoin the England squad. I grabbed a lift with Gareth Maclure, who lives nearby. The Bath boys who needed to catch the same flight took a cab. I was slightly concerned when there was no sign of Tindall, Perry, Balshaw or Catt when I arrived. I wasn't early – I don't like to leave too long to hang around ahead of take-off. However, they duly sloped in and we spent the time avoiding talking about rugby and the game.

The second opponent in our Six Nations adventure was Italy. This was a difficult game for us because we were expected to win by a landslide. Having joined the tournament the previous season, the Azzurri were visiting Twickenham for the first time in the championship.

Italian clubs had struggled in the Heineken Cup – L'Aquila and Roma had lost all their matches – but I felt that didn't tell the full story. Treviso, arguably Italy's best club side, were involved in the Shield in our group while many of the national team's top players were based abroad, including Luca Martin at Northampton. They had gone well in a 41–22 defeat by Ireland first up and although they would miss the injured Diego Dominguez and the suspended Alessandro Troncon, I knew from personal experience what we could expect early on. In Rome the previous season, we had taken some big hits and been knocked out of our stride before a rapid hat-trick from Austin Healey had helped us pull away.

Dan Luger's injury meant Austin was promoted to start the game this time, which in turn brought Jason Robinson on to the bench. He was the one everyone was talking about. Jason had played barely 10 games for Sale since switching from rugby league, and one A team game when he hadn't really touched the ball, but I knew what he was capable of. All my videos of rugby league tries seemed to feature Jason in action.

He had achieved so much already in his career, it seemed wrong to treat him like a new boy. I mean, how could I try to come across as a senior colleague? Although it was odd, the fact that he turned out to be such a feet-on-the-floor type of guy made it a lot easier. I remember when Jim Naylor went on loan from Newcastle to Halifax Blue Sox, the rugby league lads called him a 'rah-rah' but there was none of that sort of thing with Jason. The only stick he attracted was some good-

Knocking about with brother Mark at our parents' home in Farnham.

Our house in Corbridge is geared up for a life of post-rugby comfort, with its big black leather chairs and plenty of non-rugby videos to keep us entertained.

Tackled by Martin Corry in our hard-fought match against Leicester at the start of the season. Rob Andrew made his views known after the game, when he accused the Tigers of killing the ball.

In action at Bath, where we lost 19-12 after a battle to get there because of the petrol blockade and a battle on the pitch.

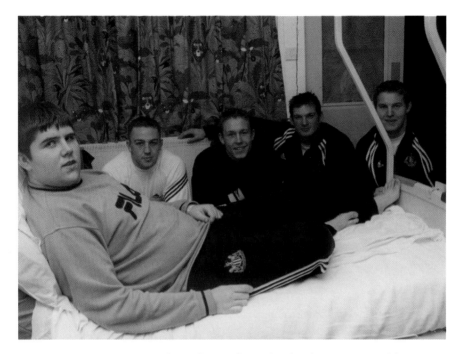

An important part of our job as professional rugby players is to spread the
word and to put something back into the local community.
Here we are visiting a local hospital around Christmas.

On a freezing cold day just after
Christmas, Gary Armstrong and I
make sure there is no way through
for Bristol's Lee Best as we start
a run of seven straight victories.

Empics

Not my greatest kicking day at the Tetley's Bitter Cup final against Harlequins, where we scraped home with a last-minute try.

After a final as dramatic as that one, the celebrations were always going to be a bit special.

A wonderful moment. I felt a great sense of achievement –

the Falcons were showing signs of their potential.

On the way to the PRA awards ceremony with my mum.

Being presented with the Player of the Year shield later the same evening by Mick Cleary of the *Daily Telegraph*.

Rob Andrew has helped me so much in my career. Here he reminds me that I am close to overhauling his record as England's top points scorer.

The neck problem that plagued me towards the end of the season finally forces me off the pitch during the Falcons' last league game, against Saracens, as we ended up a disappointing sixth.

Deep in thought.

Newcastle's home strip, the best-looking in the Premiership – unlike the bloke wearing it!

natured ribbing about his salary from Austin who reckoned he owned south Manchester and re-named the area Jasonville.

He had plenty to learn, calls wise, in a short space of time and although we had no idea whether he would get on the pitch, most of the media seemed to be speculating that he would make an appearance. Mike Catt was also in demand with the press because he was due to win his 50th England cap, which meant leading the team out.

I had a few interviews to do, including one with Sky. Graham Simmons, the interviewer, took me unawares by asking about Valentine's Day. It fell on the Wednesday before the game and he wanted to know how many cards I had sent and received. The answers were none and two. Enticing that special someone to join you for a romantic Valentine's evening retrieving muddy rugby balls at kicking practice takes some doing.

I had no soul-mate at Pennyhill Park either. Dan Luger's absence meant a suite to myself. Although I often enjoy my own company, I had grown quite accustomed to having him around and it was different being on my own. In search of colleagues, I headed down to the team massage room. This had become an unofficial meeting place for the players where we got together to chat or watch a video or a quiz show on TV. 'The Weakest Link', 'Fifteen To One' and 'Countdown' are popular, particularly with Martin Johnson.

The massage room has a soothing, therapeutic quality about it and is a great place to chill out. After Wednesday morning training, I went along and met up with Mike Tindall. It did not take long for the room's magic spell to take effect. In no time at all we were dozing, blissfully sleeping away the pressures of international week.

I was woken by what sounded like a pneumatic drill going off near my ear. Tindall's snoring was disturbing my peace, good and proper. The only explanation I could find for its devastating power was the damage to Mike's nose. It has been broken so many times that it must be a hell of a job for the air to make it through to his lungs and back out again.

We had studied Italy's opening game against Ireland and had a brief talk about what we thought they might do against us. After the way we had played against Wales, we thought Italy might try to block up the wide channels we had used so successfully in Cardiff. In Rome the previous year, they had made it difficult to attack so we were keen to ensure we had other options if we needed them. I wanted to be sure of what would happen in each sector of the pitch so I asked Johnno to set up a series of scrums and lineouts in certain positions so we could go through the moves we would use from there.

All the key decision-makers have an input in training. As captain, Johnno always liaises with the likes of Matt Dawson, Lawrence Dallaglio and me over what we want to be doing. The important thing the coaches were keen to stress was adaptability. You can practise all you want but if the opposition fills one hole or leaves another open, a side must be able to exploit it on the spur of the moment. It makes no sense to run into brick walls all afternoon.

I was confident England had players who were flexible. The pace we had in the back three meant it made sense for us to use that but if, for instance, the weather dictated we should play a tighter game, we had proved we could do that too. Our pack can get around the pitch well but they are also strong.

Ideally, against Italy we wanted to play with the ball. How it is presented at the tackle is important to the continuity needed to play this type of game and this was an area our head coach, Andy Robinson, was keen to look at. Using a video of the game against Wales, he singled out Austin for an excellent piece of ball presentation in contact. He said it was very good, especially for the smallest person in the team. Austin prides himself on his strength so we were all delighted with this description and immediately gave him a new nickname – 'Tiny Tim'. It was to be put up in lights.

When drivers make their way up the long, leafy drive to Pennyhill Park, they are greeted by a computerised sign flashing up their number plate and the word 'welcome'. It is a security measure but quite a neat trick nonetheless. Before training, Austin had asked one of the hotel's staff to change the message so that when he arrived it would flash up 'welcome, Austin' instead. When he returned with a car full of team-mates, it dutifully gave its personalised greeting, much to his delight.

After Andy Robinson's comments, Will Greenwood was seen having a word in the ear of the security man. When Austin returned from training the next day with another car full, he drew his passengers' attention to the sign as they got closer. But instead of his ego receiving another massage, it was crushed as the computer flashed up 'welcome, Tiny Tim'.

However, Austin was soon back on top of the world. He was voted man of the match against Italy after scoring two of our 10 tries in a record 80–23 win.

Matters had looked a good deal different at half-time when we led 33–23 but we were pleased with how we pulled things together in the second half. We showed a lot of professionalism in identifying our problems and what we needed to do to sort them out, and then putting that into practice.

Half-time works a bit like this: when we go in we change our kit, drink water or isotonic drinks, and have a quiet couple of minutes to ourselves to calm down and reflect dispassionately on the first half. Clive and Brian Ashton talk to the backs, Andy Robinson to the forwards. Phil Larder divides his time between the two. I often shuttle between the two groups as well, discussing what has worked, what hasn't, and what we need to do in the second half.

Clive writes a few points on a board, simple triggers that we can take on board immediately – keep hold of the ball, put them on the floor in the tackle, that sort of thing. He may jot down a specific lineout or open-field ploy as well. The coaches go over these points and then are able to leave the room.

In our final couple of minutes before we go out, Johnno will make sure we know what we are doing especially at the kick-off and prepare us mentally for the physical battering to come. There is no shouting or bawling but you cannot go out on to the field in a relaxed state.

For a fly-half it was an interesting test because there are no hard or fast rules about what to expect from the Italian defenders. Sometimes my opposite number, Giovanni Raineri, and his inside-centre, Walter Pozzebon, were up on me like greyhounds; other times they hung back. So it was a question of finding space and then capitalising on it.

We were doing the right things in the first half but were a bit careless with the ball. We tended to become over-excited in try-scoring areas and made the wrong decisions. At the interval we decided we needed to be more clinical and composed. We didn't do much differently after the break although we were a little bit more direct at the start, but we just did everything better. It helped that Pozzebon was sin-binned in the 55th minute – that gave us some more space – but even when he returned tries were scored.

Joe Worsley got off the bench to score one, which was a good end to an up-and-down week for him. Before the match, he had confessed over dinner to having seen himself on a gay porn Internet site. It was, he insisted, his face grafted on to someone else's body although it was apparently quite a flattering physique. Joe said he had innocently typed in the words 'rugger buggers' and discovered this sordid site.

There was another high-profile substitute appearance, too. Jason Robinson came on for his international rugby union debut but whatever he did, the ball just would not go his way. I tried everything I could to get possession to him but he was always one pass away from the ball. I joked afterwards that he was the best decoy runner I'd ever seen. In the end, Jason barged Matt Dawson out of the way, picked up the ball from a ruck and danced his way through the tacklers to leave his imprint on the game. I thought that was awesome. A lot of people in his position with his lack of experience in a new game would have been happy enough just to have a safe debut and get through it. Jason made a statement of intent in doing what he did.

You could understand how he must have been frustrated. Even I managed to score a try near the end. I thought I was in just beforehand but Italy gave away a penalty. A quick tap allowed Mike Catt to take out most of the defence with a pass which gave me a clear run to the line. People said there was a special cheer for my try but although I heard the decibel level go up I was already turning my attention to the conversion so there wasn't much time to soak up the reception. The kick took my tally to 13 out of 13 for the day and set a new Six Nations record of 35 points in a match.

However, I missed the last conversion from near the left-hand touchline when Lawrence Dallaglio scored, which was annoying. The pitch at Twickenham was a touch bare at the spot I would have chosen so I had to take the kick from closer to the try-line than I wanted. That made the angle narrower. It was no excuse – I should have slotted it anyway.

Although my try was enjoyable and the kicking successes satisfying, particularly early on when the teams were neck and neck, the real highlight of my day was probably a tackle I made on Mauro Bergamasco. It came as early as the second minute and put a marker down for the side. It helped to get us into the game.

Bergamasco picked up the ball in his own half and ran straight at me, which gave me plenty of time to set up for the tackle. Because I'm not that big, people seem to want to knock me over by running at me. Sometimes they do, but not this time. I went quite high, launching myself at Bergamasco and whacking him in the chest. The impact stopped the Italian flanker in his tracks and was replayed endlessly by Sky. I had to go high because of the angle at which he was coming at me; otherwise I would have got his arm and knee in my face. I aimed for the ball to try to dislodge it but slipped up a little higher and his head whipped back on impact. There was no doubt it was a fair tackle.

I love big hits. I used to watch rugby league when I was little for the clattering challenges, and when I started playing club rugby at centre, I decided to try to be equally strong in the tackle and hold my ground. That is something I have developed at international level. If I watch a game I have been playing in, I've no interest in replaying the kicks or the good decisions, only the tackles or open-field running.

The hit I made on Emile Ntamack against France the previous season was another particularly satisfying one. In the context of a tight game in Paris, a resounding tackle on one of their key men just before half-time was psychologically important. There is a wall outside the Twickenham dressing room filled with plaques commemorating great England wins. The Ntamack tackle is mentioned there.

I have made a fair few others at club level which have been equally enjoyable but which have not been shown to as wide an audience. I tried to make a compilation tape of some of them to use if my confidence was low – a sort of greatest hits album – but sadly the technology proved too much and I ended up with footage of a lot of rucks.

Although I love the physical confrontation, you have to be realistic. There is no point starting something you cannot finish. Sometimes you have to settle for making a safe tackle and putting your opponent on the ground. There is not much to be gained from trying to take out someone such as Richard Metcalfe, Scotland's 7ft 1in and 20st lock. It makes more sense to tackle him low and allow the side to compete for the ball on the ground. I make up my mind pretty early and then go for it. It's always worth remembering that if you go in for a big tackle in the wrong position, it can be dangerous. Nevertheless, there is nothing like a crunching tackle to lift a side.

We left Twickenham in happy mood that night, ready to return a fortnight later for the Calcutta Cup game against Scotland. But before then, Jason Leonard, Will Greenwood and I would be back for one of the games of the season – Harlequins versus Newcastle in the Tetley's Bitter Cup final.

chapter eight

Walking in a Walder wonderland

G oing back to Twickenham with my Newcastle team-mates for the Cup final was a fantastic feeling. Playing there for England was one thing but to step out with the guys from the club with whom I spend most of my time was somehow different. We are friends as well as workmates and that made it extra special.

The average age of the Newcastle side captured a lot of attention ahead of the final. Apart from me, the backs included Dave Walder, Jamie Noon, Tom May and Michael Stephenson, who were all English, talented and under 23. Yet when *Rugby World* magazine lined up a picture of the Falcons' gifted youngsters, I wasn't included. I seemed to be bracketed differently.

To a certain extent I am caught between two stools. Having been at Newcastle for four years, I got to know the first-generation Falcons well. George Graham, Doddie and Gary Armstrong were my initial friends at the club. The younger guys who were beginning to make such an impact all came through the Northumbria University system and naturally knocked around together. While most of them live in

Jesmond, which is a stone's throw from the heart of Newcastle, I'm out in the sticks near Corbridge and don't have their student life.

I am a little bit jealous. On a rare weekend off two years ago I went along with a few of them to Dublin and had a fantastic time. But the fact that England happened so early for me was bound to put me in a parallel existence for at least some of the time. Sometimes I feel I don't spend enough time with my contemporaries. It is great to be with them whenever I can. I'll go to the cinema a couple of times a week with the likes of Dave Walder or just hang out with them at the club or at restaurants.

The younger element live in a different world from the old-timers and as you might expect there is plenty of baiting between the two groups. It was summed up well by Jamie Noon in an article he wrote for one of our programmes. It read:

Having accepted my promotion to club journalist, as part of my research I set about interviewing the younger lads. They all felt it was about time that the fans knew the truth about the suffering us young guys have to put up with behind the scenes.

There is an unspoken policy in most clubs to wind up and disrespect the younger lads so I have compiled evidence to gain sympathy and some understanding for the young guns.

Our grief begins in the changing rooms every morning. We are all bullied and herded into a corner and struggle to change with bums in team-mates' faces. Not only that, but we have to put up with the smelly, hairy Jim Jenner changing in front of us. Torture.

On away trips, so that we don't get complacent, we are treated like slaves by the godfathers of the Falcons (Weir, Armstrong, Walton, Nesdale) and ordered to supply a continuous stream of tea and coffee.

'Refuse,' I hear you say. 'Just say no to bullies.' A few have attempted to strike and have had to succumb to the worst punishment – fines. The old school (Rob, Richard Arnold, Doddie and Batesy) take our hard-earned cash to fuel eating and drinking binges at the end of the season, which they name Mad Monday. It has been rumoured that Doddie has an offshore bank account that he keeps topping up with our money for his retirement.

Due to the heavy fines, the young guns all have to rent property together to save enough money to eat. For example, Massey, Mower and Ian Peel live together; Hall Charlton and Tom sleep rough with students; Stevo and Ross Cook share a bed (oops, bedsit); Wardy can't leave home and Epi shares a cardboard box in Eldon Square. In comparison, the Corbridge mafia (Doddie, Sparks and JW) are sitting pretty in their big houses.

The youngsters recently formed an alliance; headquarters are in the Jesmond area of Newcastle. To stifle any sort of revolution, the old school along with the Corbridge mafia, burgled an essential meeting place, Tom's house. While the young guns were dozing, in crept the mafia. Luckily for us, Batesy licked his fingers which alerted the nightwatchman.

The following night, the young guns locked every door and window in the house and nailed down all the adult mags to prevent Walts stealing them. As suspected, the mafia returned, this time using Doddie's ears as a catapult to fire rocks at our first line of defence. As a final measure of strength, the mafia employed their secret yet deadly weapon – Wilkinson banter.

There's plenty more where that came from but I'm sure you get the general idea. Behind the rivalry is a deep bond of camaraderie and I think that was what pulled us through the tough times in our Cup odyssey. It began back in November.

Strangely, the fourth and fifth rounds were drawn at the same time. That meant the fifth-round draw read (Barking or Rosslyn Park) or Newcastle v. Bristol or Wasps – clear as mud. To reach that stage it turned out we had to beat Rosslyn Park from two divisions below us. It should have been a banker but we had been drawn away from home and there is always the Cup factor to take into account. Cup rugby feels different. There is a special tingle of anticipation about a tie whether it is the minnow taking on the Premiership club or between the big clubs themselves. The sure knowledge that there are no second chances gives the games an alternative flavour. Win and you are through; lose and that's it.

Facing a Premiership club meant a great day for Rosslyn Park and an opportunity to show what the club could offer to people who would not normally go to watch. They certainly impressed me from the bench. Part-time players they may have been but they had a lot of the game and made up for any lack of fitness with an overdose of adrenaline. They made us sweat for a 25–13 win.

Matches like this are difficult for the favourites because everyone expects them just to turn up and win. It's not as simple as that. We had to be very professional and make sure we kept that fear of losing; otherwise our Cup run could have ended there and then.

When I saw the complex initial draw, I expected to be facing Wasps in the fifth round, not because there was anything wrong with Bristol but it just seemed the two clubs were magnetically attracted in the Cup. We seemed to get them every year. Bristol's removal of the holders meant we had to plan for a different type of side. They were struggling a bit in the league but they had a big pack who could intimidate us early on if we let them. We were also aware we had to watch out for their electric scrum-half Agustin Pichot, and try not to concede penalties because in Steve Vile they possessed a good kicker.

I was back in the side for what turned out to be a tight match. Every time we made a break their cover defence stopped us turning it into a try, so although we eventually crossed through Andy Mower and Gary Armstrong, in the end it came down to goalkicking. Fortunately, it was my day. I managed eight out of eight including a 55 metre penalty – the longest of my career – and we came through a stiff test.

The quarter-final draw handed us another Premiership team, London Irish, but also another home draw. Beating Irish was a fine performance. We had played them five days beforehand in the league and lost so we wanted to erase that memory. The match featured a rare Wilkinson try. Like anyone, I love scoring them but while some people seem to have the knack of being in the right place at the right time, I don't. So scoring a try that makes a difference, like the one against Irish, is all the more special.

We were narrowly ahead, 16–10, early in the second half when we were offered a straightforward opportunity after Irish conceded a penalty near their own posts. It was the sort of kick I should have knocked over in my sleep. I looked up and saw they weren't defending the left-hand side of the pitch very well and a lightbulb lit up above my head. At the same time, Andy Mower and Inga realised what was on and shouted across to me. I stage whispered out of the side of my mouth to let them know I had seen the gap – there was no point telling Irish as well – and when Gary Armstrong slung the ball across to me I made the decision to take a quick tap.

Suddenly I spotted Paul Sackey, one of the fastest players in the game, closing in and it crossed my mind that if he pinned his ears back he could make me look a real chump. Spurning a kickable opportunity and messing up a tap would not have gone down well with the rest of the team. Fortunately, Sackey and the other Irish defenders went out left to cover Inga and allowed me to go through the hole to the try-line without anyone laying a finger on me. I tried to look as if I wasn't relieved afterwards but I don't think I got away with it.

I've pulled off that sort of stunt once before, for England against Queensland in 1999. That time the gamble wasn't as great because the penalty had been awarded on our 22 but it paid dividends with Leon Lloyd streaking away to score at the other end.

Taking quick taps is a risky business but it is an opportunity to catch a defence with its trousers down. Matt Dawson is a master at the art. It doesn't always work but when it does, a seven-pointer is a real bonus.

We had to overcome an unsettling few moments when Gareth Maclure was stretchered off in a neck brace – he was OK after a check-up at the hospital. Then we played some decent rugby and scored tries through Liam and Inga. Irish fought back at the end after Richard Arnold had been sin-binned for the fifth time in four months, but we were pretty good value for our win and a place in the semi-final.

Leicester were the side everyone was keen to avoid in the last four after their quarter-final win over Saracens, and when Sale came out of the hat we felt that was as favourable a draw as we could have hoped for. It was to be played at Kingston Park, which was crucial, particularly the way our season was dividing into home wins and away losses – at least it looked like it was Kingston Park. Our name had been pulled out first so, logically, we presumed that meant we would host the game – not so. The RFU announced they were thinking of staging a double header, that is both semi-finals would be played on the same day at the same ground. The Madejski Stadium seemed to be their preferred option.

While Reading was handy for Harlequins supporters and not too bad for Leicester, it would have meant a long journey for Newcastle and Sale fans. Headingley was talked about as an alternative, which would have suited the sponsors, Tetley's, as their beer is brewed just down the road. But the double-header idea was eventually rejected after Rob protested.

There was still a hurdle to clear to bring the game to Kingston Park as all semi-final venues had, for some reason, to have an 8,000 capacity. A planning application had been submitted aimed at turning Kingston Park into a 10,000 capacity ground but as things stood, our limit fell just short. We felt sure that for a one-off it could be raised, if that was necessary.

The RFU deferred a decision until the day after our quarter-final, which gave our owner Dave Thompson the opportunity to let off some steam. He was characteristically forthright about what he thought of the whole process. In the end, the RFU relented and it turned out to be a great occasion for Kingston Park and Newcastle rugby. Sky do not venture into the north east too often but they were here that day. There were plenty of journalists too, and the crowd of 6,257 was our biggest for years. The place was buzzing.

We were so close to Twickenham and we knew a big performance would get us there but we could not afford to think beyond Sale. There is so much at stake in semi-finals that they are almost like finals themselves. If you lose, it is no different from going out in the fourth round – no one remembers you.

The management chose to leave out Liam Botham, which was a tough call but it just showed how competitive selection had become among the backs. Rob wanted to play Michael Stephenson and with Dave Walder at full-back that left no room for Liam.

Sale were in form but we had studied them the previous week when they lost to Bristol in the league and had noted their lineout problems. Our forwards did a great job in exploiting that deficiency and they lost almost half a dozen on their own throw in the first half hour of the game. That made a big difference for me because it meant I could kick the ball into touch knowing we had an acceptable chance of winning it back on their throw. Unless we are under tremendous pressure, I usually try to keep the ball in play so the opponents are forced to put it out and concede the throw-in.

The presence of Jason Robinson was another factor in our kicking game – the chase was so important in closing him down. I had seen some of his work with the ball in hand on television – in the build-up to the match, Sky showed some of the best Super League tries. That reinforced how important it was for me to measure my kicking and not give him chances to counter-attack. We managed it fairly well although he demonstrated just how dangerous he can be when he was given half an opportunity in the second half and beat three men. Fortunately for me, he slipped just before he reached me. I dived on top of him as if to say 'and don't try that again, or else'.

In the first half we played some fine rugby and should have wrapped up the game by the interval but Tom May's two tries proved conclusive in the end. Tom scored a 27th minute try after a quick tap by Dave Walder, which put us in the clear at 23–3, and then a cracker 16 minutes into the second half. After taking the ball off Bryan Redpath's toe, he shrugged off three tacklers on a 40 metre sprint to the corner and gestured to his flatmates in the crowd as he scored.

Sale came back with two tries in five minutes from Duncan Bell and Steve Hanley but even though we had Richard Arnold sin-binned again for a stamp, they had too much to do.

It felt great to win the semi-final – the reception we received on our lap of honour was terrific. People often ask me if I enjoyed a particular match. The truth is I don't consciously enjoy the game itself – I'm too busy trying to do as much as I can right. What I enjoy is looking back at it. This time I had mixed feelings after the euphoria and the last chorus of 'Blaydon Races' – word perfect after our pre-season choral training in Narbonne – had died away. It was a relief to be in the final but I hadn't played the game I wanted. OK, my goalkicking went well in windy conditions and I scored 22 points, but the rest of my game was not really up to the standards I set myself. Important games should bring out the best in me. This one hadn't.

There are two sides to me as a rugby player – the meticulous individual who works hard in training, and the matchday performer. The second deals with the pressure and repays the first for all the graft, discomfort, time and effort I put in. I was disappointed because I had done a lot of practice on drop goals during the week but I messed up

On the floor against the Wallabies in November – I promise it wasn't
due to the nightmare journey from hell by taxi to get there.

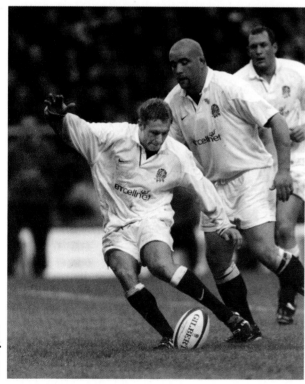

My drop goal in a
tense victory against
Australia – I was to
see much more of them
before the year was out.

With the Cook Cup and Dan Luger, the man whose injury-time try
against the Wallabies won it.

The game that nearly didn't happen: the England squad had
unanimously threatened to withdraw from the match against Argentina,
but once it was on we were focused entirely on winning.

Making a break through the midfield against the Springboks
in another very high-intensity Test.

Celebrations in the back of the bus after we'd beaten South Africa. It was
a privilege to be invited into the front row's domain.

On the burst and evading two flying tackles.

Enjoying my first taste of the Millennium Stadium attempting to escape the clutches of Rob Howley, who was to become a firm friend on the Lions tour.

With fellow Lions Matt Dawson, Neil Back and Richard Hill in the hotel lobby after England's victory over Wales.

Mike Catt's pass opens the way for me against Italy as England pulled away in the second half.

Where I like it best – in the thick of the action against Italy.

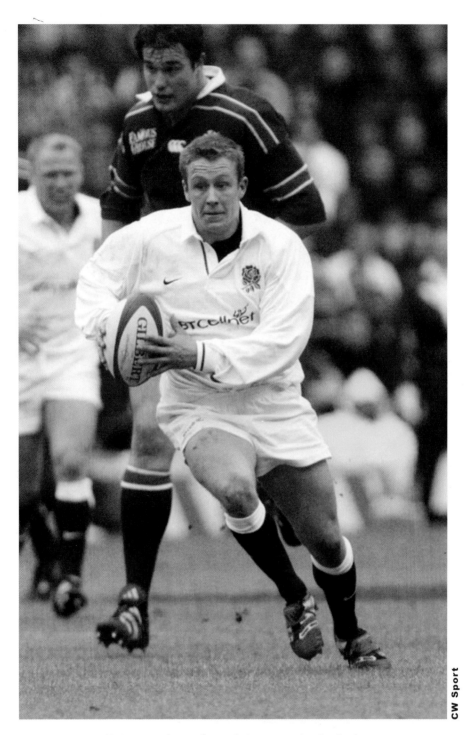

Trying to work out what to do in space against Scotland.

Trying to turn the pressure back on France, who
gave us a real fright.

Going for goal as I overtake
Rob Andrew's record to
become England's top
points scorer. I only
realised I'd done it when I
heard the announcement
going in at half time.

two chances to put us 15 points and three scores clear. I had knocked them over hundreds of times in training.

I also indirectly cost the side a try in the first half by putting a clearance kick straight into the grateful arms of Steve Hanley. Charlie Hodgson scored a couple of phases later. Again, I had spent ages practising this sort of thing only for the execution to go awry when it mattered.

Some people might class these as minor errors but to me, even though we won, they were important. I put them straight out of my mind during the game – you have to – but afterwards, because of these mistakes, I was quiet as we celebrated.

I was able to have a laugh, though, when Doddie levied a stiff fine on Gareth Maclure after taking exception to his shoes. Gareth hadn't even been playing – he'd only come in to congratulate us.

Ross Beattie, who scored our first try, broke a bone in his neck during the semi-final although we didn't realise it at the time. He wanted to carry on playing but he couldn't. The injury was confirmed a couple of weeks later so we lost his services for the remainder of the season. It was his second setback in quick succession. He had sustained a serious injury to his pride in training. The incident concerned Liam Botham.

Liam is extremely health conscious and has recovery drinks waiting in the changing room after every practice session. On this occasion, he plonked them down in Ross's space so Ross wasn't able to sit down. Ross had a sense of humour failure and angrily chucked Liam's drinks in the bin before returning to the field for a forwards' session. When Liam came in and found them he naturally wanted to know who was responsible. Being honourable sorts, we all immediately told him it was Ross and started firing him up for revenge.

Revved up, Liam picked up Ross's underpants – a brave move in itself – and rubbed Deep Heat cream into them. We convinced him that this could hardly be classified as adequate retribution so he got hold of Ross's socks and cut the toes off with a pair of scissors. Not bad, we told him, but you still need to do more. Liam dutifully opened up a tub of Vaseline and put a handful into each of Ross's brand new shoes.

Ross eventually returned from training, showered and put on his pants. He had recently broken his nose and being an occasionally vain sort was concerned about his good looks. Perhaps being named in a list of the most eligible bachelors in Scotland had gone to his head. Anyway, dressed in just his pants, he was checking for any permanent disfigurement in the mirror when the scratching started. It worsened as he went over to talk to Marten Brewer, our physio.

Soon after he was in pain and, confronted by a row of faces desperately trying not to laugh, it dawned on him what had happened. He hastily took the offending pants off and put his trousers on instead. Then he decided to put on his socks but when he tried to pull one up it ended up covering his knee. By now, he was annoyed. He had a fair idea of who was responsible and decided to go out to find him. He slid his sock-less foot into his shoe and found Vaseline sliding out from between his toes.

'Botham,' he shouted. Ross threatened revenge on a massive scale, but his injuries distracted him and, in the end, Liam escaped.

The Cup final had been shifted to 24 February to create a hole for the new end-of-season play-offs. Picking possibly the coldest month of the year represented a big change and with Harlequins playing Newcastle in the showpiece, the pundits were predicting a low crowd. I had some sympathy with that view. The Twickenham final had a distinct atmosphere partly because it was an end-of-season party in the sunshine for supporters. I used to go every year as a child.

I played there in a curtain-raiser in 1990 – the year Bath beat Gloucester – for Farnham Under-11s. It was a scorching day and we were running around gasping for drinks. We sat in awe afterwards, realising just how fit and strong these players must be.

Moving the Cup climax to midwinter took some getting used to but it was better than the alternative – no Cup at all. That was what was being considered during the endless deliberations between the RFU and the top clubs. I was glad when its future was secured. I mean, imagine football doing away with the FA Cup. The club knockout competition has a special place in English rugby. It is difficult to imagine a season without it.

Losing two years previously against Wasps had hurt but it was a wonderful day out for thousands of Newcastle fans who came down to Twickenham to support us. That sense of enjoyment filtered through to the players. This time we were determined to send them on the long journey home happy. The club played their part by getting local businesses to sponsor buses down to London so people were able to travel for £1. Over 10,000 went down from the north east and fears about a half-empty stadium were allayed with a fantastic 71,000 attendance.

A lot of people were surprised that Quins had made it through to the final, given their struggles in the league. We knew they were dangerous, as Leicester found out in the semi-final when they were outplayed up front. Not many teams do that to the Tigers. They had also beaten Northampton along the way. We were a young team still finding our way so to reach Twickenham was a fine achievement. But now we were there, I desperately wanted to win.

The whole week felt different. Everyone in Newcastle seemed to be talking about the final. We had team photos taken, a big press day and flew down for the game. We were issued with brand new outfits, even down to boxer shorts. I'm a long boxers kind of man myself and was quite happy with what arrived, but the boys who ordered the short type looked like they were in swimming trunks from the 1970s. The suits were spot on, though.

At our final meeting before departure, Rob Andrew decreed that we had to wear our club leisure wear, which he was already wearing, to travel down in.

'I want you to look like this,' he said, pointing at himself. Jamie Noon put up his hand.

'Can we part our hair differently or does it have to be to the left?' he asked.

When the team was announced, the losers were Richard Arnold, who was left out for Rob Devonshire, and Liam. The writing had been on the wall for Liam perhaps when he was on the bench for the Bath game, but this was the one no one wanted to miss and I felt for him. I've been a substitute enough times to know how it feels. When you win, however much people include you, it still feels hollow if you have not contributed directly on the pitch.

Liam took it professionally but it was a difficult time for him. Having played and performed well in every game until January his appearances were then restricted first because of selection and then injury. His season petered out towards the end, really. For someone whose arrival had been so high-profile, it must have been difficult to deal with. But he did deal with it, and very well. He will be back, of that I'm sure. He works so hard and has such a lot of talent that it is almost impossible to imagine him failing. The consolation for Liam at the Cup final was being part of a wonderful occasion – George Graham missed out totally because of his calf injury.

Va'aiga Tuigamala was a doubt too but he put off an elbow operation to play. He could not miss the game because it gave a national audience the chance to savour his remarkable new haircut. Usually near-bald, Inga's head resembled a mafia-like microphone that day. Six weeks earlier, Inga had entered into a bet with Rob. For some reason, he was practising place-kicking from the in-goal area and it was going predictably badly. Optimistically, he decided to wager his own hair against Rob's that he would kick the next one from a tricky angle. He would grow his if he missed it; Rob would shave his off if he kicked it. He was nowhere near. Whether it was the hair that proved inspirational I don't know, but Inga was the man of the match in the final, which was a remarkable effort given he could not move or feel anything in two of his fingers.

What a game it was! For Newcastle to come back at the finish and score two tries to snatch the Cup was extraordinary. To do so on the back of one of my least favourite kicking displays of the season – in fact, of all my seasons – was testament to the performances of the rest of the side. Harlequins must have thought they had it won, 27–18 up coming into the home straight, but we kept our heads and backed ourselves to do what we needed to. The rugby we had endeavoured to play all season was meant for a situation like this and in the wide open spaces of Twickenham it was my job to make sure we kept playing it. Perspective was everything. If we panicked, we would lose.

As Quins tired we kept attacking them wide, trusting our handling and support play and hoping cracks would eventually appear. They did. In the 76th minute, a turnover in the right-hand corner gave Jim Jenner the opportunity to score wide out on the left after Inga had been held up just short.

That brought the score to 27–23 with the conversion to come. I thought I had struck the kick perfectly but it drifted just wide. We still had to score a try to win the game. It was my fourth miss of the afternoon and potentially crucial.

Amid the tension, the noise of the crowd and the stream of messages being relayed on to the pitch, I had to put my disappointment to one side and clear my head. We had somehow to get back up to the other end of the pitch and work an opening from which to score again.

Paul Burke kicked long and we ran the ball back at Quins. I moved the ball wide out to the left where Inga barrelled his way into their half. We had the position we needed but we still had to carve out a try-scoring opportunity.

As the clock moved on to 80 minutes, Will Greenwood went down injured. We asked the referee Ed Morrison, who was making his last Twickenham appearance, how much injury time was left. It was just under four minutes.

Quins had control of the ball but Gary Armstrong managed to tie up possession, giving us the scrum put-in. We probed out on the right before bringing the ball left where Ian Peel, our substitute prop, made a charge for the corner. He was bundled into touch by a desperate tackle from Paul Burke but as he made the tackle, the Quins fly-half ripped the ball away, or so touch judge Steve Lander thought. It was a controversial call because it meant we had the throw-in to the lineout five metres from the Quins line.

Ross Nesdale threw to Stuart Grimes near the tail and the forwards went for the drive but were held up. Initially, I called a short move in the backs but as the forwards went for a second surge I changed my mind. Usually when a team is defending on their own line, they have an extra metre to get up into the tackle so it can be unwise to spread the play wide. However, this time Will Greenwood had been sucked in to help near the maul and Quins' defence had been drawn in so I opted to go for it, knowing that a side-on tackle from them would not be enough to stop us scoring.

I called to Gary Armstrong for quick ball and he delivered it. When the ball arrived I missed out Tom May and spun it wide to Jamie Noon who held the defence and put Dave Walder through the gap for the winning try. There was pandemonium. I couldn't get to him quickly enough. We had won it with the last play of the game. I had to put over the conversion from wide out, purely to be fair to myself, and as I did it I leapt for joy. The whistle blew to end one of the best finals in history.

Standing there on the touchline, I thought about throwing my kicking tee into the crowd as a celebration. It hadn't served me very well, after all. However, the spectators are quite a way back from the pitch at Twickenham and I was worried my throw might not reach. It would have been embarrassing to have to fetch it and then have another go. In the end I kept hold of it.

As I turned to the crowd, the first person I saw running towards me was Sparks. It was a very special moment when he reached me. In front of 71,000 it could not have been more public, but at the same time it was intensely private. It wasn't just the fact that we are so close, although that was important, but the knowledge of the role Sparks had played in Newcastle's and my success. He knew what it all meant.

As I took my turn to pick up the trophy, near the back of the team, I felt a great sense of achievement. It wasn't so much the Cup but what it stood for that mattered. It was tangible proof that Newcastle had been the best team in the tournament – not Leicester, not Bath, Newcastle. We were Tetley's Bitter Cup champions, and in my view we deserved it. Some people may say we had an easy draw but we had to beat four Premiership sides on the trot to win the competition and that takes some doing.

After all the elation it was depressing to walk straight into a barrage of questions from the press about missed goalkicks. Couldn't they have focused on something more positive? Newcastle, with a team of fantastic young English talent, had just won the Cup and all they could ask about was me supposedly having a poor match. I hadn't – it was just that the kicking to them was the most noticeable part of my performance. I was really pleased with the decisions I had made when they had to be spot on at the end, and with my contribution and execution of skills around the field. I would happily have told them about the effort and anxiety involved in rescuing a game from the grave, and about how personally satisfied I was. In any case, this wasn't about me; it was about the club and the occasion. For someone like Va'aiga Tuigamala, blood dripping from his nose, to describe it as the best final he had ever been involved in says a lot.

Yet I had to face facts. When the heat had been turned up on one of the most important days of my career, I had not kicked as well as I wanted and knew I could. Why had I messed up? Because I wanted it too much. I would have swapped everything I have achieved in rugby so far to win that match and when things had not been going right, that had been a hell of a feeling to deal with.

We had all been through a lot at Newcastle since the Premiership was won – two and a half hard seasons spent rebuilding a club that almost died. Dragging ourselves back up there had not been easy. There had been hard times along the way, particularly the previous season when we had taken a series of beatings. But all the time we were growing as a team and as people, developing the relationships that make playing for a club so important.

Rob Andrew said afterwards that the result did not matter because of the way we had played and the effort we had given, but I disagreed. I felt it was crucial for the club that we won, both in terms of where we were going and what we had gone through to get this far. Heads had really been turned. Newcastle was back on the rugby map.

No sooner had we won the match than Rob announced the club's aim was to take the Cup to 30,000 youngsters around the north east in the year ahead. As a promotional vehicle for rugby in the region, we had a Rolls-Royce.

People could touch the trophy but they could only imagine what it had felt like at Twickenham. To triumph in such dramatic fashion gave the day a dream-like quality. If Newcastle do go on to achieve great things as we all hope, 24 February 2001 will go down as a landmark day in the club's evolution.

At our hotel in Marble Arch, we partied into the early hours with our Under-21 side, who had beaten Harlequins that morning. They are the Falcons' future – I believe that one day many of them will experience something equally special.

chapter nine

Righting wrongs

Scotland seems to be synonymous with key moments in my England career. The first time I was a replacement for England was against the Scots in 1998; then the first time I started an international was the 1999 Calcutta Cup match. Those were good days. Murrayfield 2000, on the other hand, is a date I remember with a lot of pain.

We went to Edinburgh as favourites for a grand slam clinching victory and returned with our tails between our legs. The Scots messed around with our set-piece and without secure lineout ball, life proved very difficult. It meant they could kick to touch with impunity and still have a reasonable chance of winning or ruining our possession. In the wet conditions, that was a real bonus. They read the situation well and emerged deserved 19–13 winners.

The rematch was at Twickenham and we were raring to go. The talk outside the squad was of revenge but inside, it was more a question of owing ourselves a good performance after the desperate low of Murrayfield. If we came up with one, we felt sure we would win. England were a different proposition now. The side was far more astute and better switched on about what we were trying to do and when it was wise to do it than we had been in the rain in Edinburgh. As we had shown against Italy, we were getting better at adapting on the hoof during matches.

Thinking on our feet was all very well on the pitch but I was having trouble managing off it. The squad attended a sponsors' lunch on the Monday before the Scotland game. Sponsors' events are part of our responsibility and are always better than you think they are going to be. They offer a chance to mix with different people and are a break from the normal grind. On this occasion, though, we were asked to take part in a question and answer session. As the kicker, I tend to have to field a few questions when this happens and I feel a touch nervous standing up in front of a crowded room to answer them. Everyone expects you to be witty and clever and, in my case, they are probably often disappointed.

This time one of the written questions submitted by the guests was: 'The RFU are spending one million pounds returfing Twickenham. Is this because Jonny missed a kick and, if so, does that make him precious?'

How do you answer that? I made out the question had come from my table, who had all been very nice to me beforehand, so I had a go at them in my answer for being two-faced.

There was some doubt over Neil Back's fitness because of a knee problem that had kept him out of a club match for Leicester, but he recovered and Clive was able to name an unchanged side.

The Scots were on the up. After losing a dour match in France, the Scots had produced a great comeback to draw their game against Wales a fortnight earlier. They were capable of playing some great rugby. They had pace in the back three, an extremely versatile ball-handling prop in Tom Smith and, of course, John Leslie. In the absence of Gregor Townsend, he would be a key orchestrator for them.

We monitored the weather conditions all week but there was

never much danger of a repeat of the Murrayfield monsoon. It turned out to be cold but dry.

On the night before the game, Clive gathered us all together for a team meeting. His tack was straightforward. Last year we had let ourselves down; this year we had the chance to put it right. We were shown a few video clips of the previous season's game, highlighting the despair we felt at the end. Remember the feeling, was the underlying message, and make sure it does not happen again.

In the build-up to the match, the former Scotland flanker Finlay Calder rated our centre partnership as the worst in the championship and said that if Iain Balshaw was an international full-back he was Mel Gibson. I wonder what he thought afterwards – a record England win against Scotland, Catt and Greenwood hugely influential and Balshaw all over the papers after his two tries.

The Scots caused us problems in a fiercely competitive first half but Lawrence Dallaglio's second try in injury time gave us a clear 22–3 lead at the break. I just managed to squeeze out the pass to him after committing a couple of defenders, but it was more a case of Lawrence being in the right place, just as Richard Hill had been earlier to take my pass and score out on the right wing. The Scots were tenacious, and managed to survive a sin-binning for Budge Pountney for a kick at Matt Dawson without conceding any points; but we finished strongly and were happy with some of the rugby we played in running out 43–3 winners.

There is no such thing as the perfect performance and we made mistakes, but during parts of the game we succeeded in playing as we practised, which was satisfying. Our coaches are ambitious in the way they set out the game for us to play, and are not afraid to try something new. As Clive says, if all you do is copy someone else you will never catch up with them, let alone overtake them. We had found a way to utilise the pace we had out wide, and other sides were having difficulty handling it.

Iain Balshaw, Ben Cohen and Austin Healey are all quick and then we had Jason Robinson, who is no slouch, to bring on with 20 minutes left. The way he changed direction at right angles at full tilt was incredible and he proved a big hit with the Twickenham crowd. He was even being talked about as a Lions candidate afterwards, which was amazing given that he had been playing for Wigan in Super League earlier in the season.

Being surrounded by all this pace made me feel something of a snail. I'm not blessed with unbelievable sprint ability but I try to make up for that with hard work. I spent much of the early part of my professional career working on kicking, running games and the mental part of my game. While I know I'm not the complete article yet with skills or decision-making, I am devoting more of my time to the physical side now – speed and agility. There are genetic limits to how much I can achieve but I want to squeeze as much extra as possible out of myself. Some of the boys – Dan Luger and Matt Perry, for example – have used specialist sprint coaches such as Margot Wells, the wife of former Olympic 100 metre champion Allan Wells. I use Steve Black who helps tremendously in this area.

It was pace as much as anything that beat the Scots. As well as the six tries we scored, one of the most pleasing aspects of the victory was keeping them out from our try-line. We had conceded two tries in our first two matches of the championship and knew we had to improve. We placed a lot of emphasis on defence in the build-up and it showed, particularly at the end when we could have leaked a soft try and it would not have mattered. Instead, the discipline remained right until the final whistle.

Andy Nicol, Scotland's captain, was kind enough to say we were as good a side as he had ever come up against. It was our day, I had to agree. Even when, after Balshaw's second try, I mis-hit a conversion attempt from the right-hand touchline, the kick went over. It bent both ways like a stray firework before somehow finding its way between the posts. I laughed. After all my problems the previous week at Twickenham in the Cup final, it felt like the rugby gods were on my side this time.

As we returned to our clubs, it seemed England were on a roll. Ireland should have been next up, many pundits' favourites to beat us. Instead, it was foot and mouth that did so. The first major outbreak of the disease since 1967 was detected a few miles down the road from my house in Northumberland. I knew virtually nothing about it but the farmers in our side at Newcastle spelt out how serious it could be. Peter Walton and Gary Armstrong were particularly caught up in the crisis. They both owned family sheep farms, Peter in Alnwick, Northumberland, and Gary at Jedforest in the Scottish Borders. Gary was perilously close to losing his flock at one point when the outbreak spread to within a few miles of his farm. He spent a lot of the time on away trips phoning home to check with his wife how things were. Walts suffered even worse. He had to miss one away match to help in a sheep cull at his brother's farm.

Kingston Park was right on the edge of a government exclusion zone and there was some doubt over whether it could host the A international against Scotland. In the event, the pitch was frozen and the match was switched to Headingley. Disinfected mats were put down for vehicles to drive over at our home games.

International rugby was affected more seriously. The Irish government did not want 20,000 English supporters coming over to Ireland in case the disease was carried across the Irish Sea with them, and decided our game in Dublin on 24 March had to be postponed. They had already called off Ireland's trip to Wales. The caution was understandable in the circumstances but it still came as a frustration to the players. It meant our next game, against France, was not until 7 April.

The new date earmarked for the Irish game by the Six Nations committee caused an outcry. It was 5 May, which clashed with the championship play-offs. The clubs, whose talks with the RFU were at a delicate stage, were up in arms and they insisted they would not switch the play-off dates. The decision raised the nightmare prospect of being asked to choose between club and country. I had never wanted to do anything more than play for England but as a Newcastle employee, I was duty bound to play for the club that day if I was asked. The entire club season is spent building towards the play-offs so it's unfair to ask sides to go into them without their international players.

Fortunately – or unfortunately from the farmers' point of view – we did not have to choose. The severity of the crisis eventually meant Ireland's outstanding games were put back until after the summer. The Six Nations would not be completed until October.

England's Dublin postponement meant turning our full attention to the Premiership programme for a month. Even though Leicester were cruising towards a third consecutive title, there was still everything to play for in terms of Heineken Cup qualification. The complex criteria involved meant no one knew for sure if our Tetley's Bitter Cup win would be enough to allow us in, so the league remained another avenue worth exploring. However, our Cup run had given us a headache with fixtures and we had three midweek matches to fit into a five-week period. Something had to give.

Newcastle's selection policy on our run-in caused controversy. Other clubs complained that we were devaluing the Premiership. It started against Harlequins on the Tuesday after the Scotland game. Players who had been involved in that game were given a rest by Rob whereas Quins selected Will Greenwood at centre and put Jason Leonard on the bench. A less experienced Newcastle line-up took them to the wire but Dave Walder's injury-time drop goal attempt, which would have won the match, slid wide, and Harlequins had their first league away win of the season. We had sneaked into a 22–21 lead with five minutes left but with time up, Stuart Grimes was pulled up by the referee Brian Campsall for obstructing Daren O'Leary and

Paul Burke kicked a very good penalty under presssure for Quins. It turned out to be the match winner.

Losing at home to Quins was not part of the plan and it made a victory against Sale at the weekend imperative. We picked a more familiar line-up and played our best rugby of the season. We started well, taking a 15–0 lead in a feisty opening during which Epi Taione was sin-binned for us as was Andy Morris for Sale. Sale came back at us and closed the gap to 15–10 early in the second half but after that we really cut loose.

The first half had been promising but my own performance was a little slow to start. I was determined to make an impression early in the second period and I did, breaking the Sale defence, drawing Jason Robinson and sending Jamie Noon away. Unfortunately, he pulled his hamstring and did not score but the tone was set. In one amazing purple patch, the score went from 15–10 to 48–10 in 17 minutes.

As a team we were powerful and patient; as individuals we all seemed to click. Everyone's attributes came to the fore – it was like watching a highlights video. Michael Stephenson showed his pace and balance in scoring a fantastic 60 metre try, Stuart Grimes – a great reader of the game – was everywhere in support and Tom May's power was tremendous. It is a wonderful feeling to be part of a team playing like that – you can almost feel the confidence being exuded – and we ended up scoring seven tries in a 48–24 win. I did feel slightly embarrassed, though. During the game I put in a late tackle on Jason largely because it was my only chance of making any sort of tackle on him. It wasn't so late as to give away a penalty but he had a foot off the ground at the time so he fell pretty heavily. I felt bad about what I thought was a cheap shot and for the rest of the game I tried to catch his eye to apologise. I never got the chance and ended up being collared by him after the game and being branded 'dirty'. Jason had a big grin across his face at the time.

We were playing Leicester the following Saturday at Welford Road and I was told by Rob I would not be needed until after then. The idea was for me to come back fresh and strong for other important games.

I felt at a loose end. I thought about catching a last-minute flight and going somewhere hot for a few days but because all my colleagues were still training I had no one to go with. I didn't fancy jetting off somewhere new and having to find my way around on my own – that didn't sound particularly relaxing.

I managed a couple of rounds of damp golf at Matfen – five over after 13 holes was quite pleasing after a long lay-off – but I felt guilty about taking it easy while the rest of the lads were still working hard. That thought rested heavily on my mind so I gave up and went back to the club. I even arranged some kicking sessions with Dave Alred. To be honest, I never feel able to relax properly until the end of the season.

I watched the Leicester match on television at home with Sparks, Liam and Jamie Noon but it made for depressing viewing. The Tigers blew us away in the first half and opened up a 39–7 lead. They showed just why they were about to clinch their third consecutive league title.

Although the Tigers went through the season unbeaten at Welford Road, I think what won the Premiership for them was their defence and their away form. It is fiendishly difficult to win away, as we were finding out, but Leicester, with their determination and togetherness, managed it more than most.

It was odd watching our lads on the screen. I could imagine exactly what they were thinking and feeling as they warmed up but I was 200 miles away and there was nothing I could do to help. We were swamped. We improved in the second half and conceded just 12 more points, but the four of us gave up watching the game and tried to cheer ourselves up with a visit to my stash room.

One of the advantages of being a professional sportsman is that over the years you pick up a lot of free gear. However, some of it is not

With my dad in Queensland. He was the one who broke the news to me that I had been selected to play for the Lions.

Having a game of Red Ass –
a type of non-stop table tennis with horrendous forfeits.

Sightseeing with a difference on tour with the Lions.

I made my Lions debut against Queensland Reds, a tough match that we eventually won 42-8.

Training at Brookvale Oval in preparation for the game against
New South Wales Waratahs.

The New South Wales match hit the headlines
for all the wrong reasons.

With Lions coach Graham Henry –
for some he was a controversial
choice but I found him
inspirational.

New South Wales
Country and the Lions
observe a minute's
silence for Lions liaison
officer Anton Toia.

Empics

Empics

Practising my kicking at the
Gabba in Brisbane.

Action from the first Lions Test against Australia.
I was delighted to have played a part in such a memorable victory.

Matt Dawson, moments after
kicking his winning conversion
against ACT Brumbies. The
tension of the previous few
days is clearly visible.

Snatching a moment's respite on number one court.

The second Test ended not only in defeat for the Lions but also in my

departure on a stretcher 10 minutes from the final whistle.

Luckily, I fought my way back to fitness in time for the third Test. Here I'm discussing plans with kicking coach Dave Alred.

The agonising third Test in the Olympic Stadium, Sydney, the Wallabies' backyard.

The disappointment of losing outweighed the pleasure I got from scoring

my try in the third Test.

Close, but close isn't good enough. Defeat in the third Test left me in despair.

exactly my cup of tea. Bad Stash Day, as it was christened, involved each member of our quartet being given the worst possible combination of clothes to try on before we headed off for afternoon tea at a quiet coffee shop in Corbridge.

Sparks was sporting an ice-white tennis jacket with its label still attached and hanging out, blue jeans and a cap with a huge flat peak, pointing upwards at an alarming angle. Noony wore a reflective jacket in spacesuit silver complete with similarly unstylish cap. Liam was in light blue jeans, white trainers, a long-sleeved black polo neck and a green waistcoat. He looked like a Seniors Tour golfer. I was handed some dazzlingly white baggy trousers which went perfectly with the pair of women's shoes I had to wear. They pinched badly.

Corbridge is a genteel sort of a place so there was some consternation when we appeared. Noony ordered teacakes and they came complete with an enormous slab of butter. He facetiously asked if we could have some more butter and the waitress, who was probably distracted by serving a spaceman, duly came back with another vast pot.

Noony informed me that his mum had won a signed England shirt of mine in a competition in the *Express*. I was pleased until he told me that she now slept in it. I wasn't quite sure how to take that.

I was having a number of odd experiences with fans at the time. The international matches had raised the profiles of the England players and I regularly found myself signing this and that for supporters. However, I was slightly taken aback when I opened a letter addressed to me at the club, asking me to sign some photos. This would normally have been no problem except in this case the pictures were of Iain Balshaw.

Even more disconcertingly, I received a letter from a male fan, asking me to sign some pictures. In it he complemented me on my physique and said how he wished his future partner would be like me. The pictures were of Jason Robinson. I duly passed them on to Jason but he refused to believe that I hadn't swapped the photos over myself. He still holds this against me – that and the fact that I showed them around the rest of the team beforehand.

After missing the Leicester game, I wanted to play against Wasps in our next midweek match but was surprised to be told I wasn't needed again. Rob had decided to go with some of the players who had not played so many games, and they took quite a beating from a very good Wasps side.

Although I was frustrated, I could see Rob's point of view. In my opinion, it is impossible for any international player to feature in every game during a season. The amount a match takes out of a player in terms of the physical battering and nervous exhaustion is enormous. These days it is critical to have an interchangeable squad to enable players to rest and recover from injuries. A club has to be very lucky to put its best team out every week – you only had to look at the number of players Saracens lost during the season to see that. By bringing in other players, Newcastle were trying to develop the depth in the squad that would help them in future. Unfortunately, our performances were not the best when we tried it so teams such as Leicester and Wasps were able to post big wins. The hope is that the benefits will be felt in the long term, as they were from our struggles the previous season.

I travelled down to London on the train with the team for the Wasps game but skipped the match to meet up with my parents. Sandwiched into the visit was a kicking session with Dave Alred in a stinging hailstorm at Pennyhill Park and a photo-shoot for my final batch of coaching strips in the *Express*.

Being in London gave me the opportunity to fit in some promotional work as well. There was a lunch with the HSA (Hospital Savings Association) at which I was introduced by the MC as the England full-back, and an appearance on the BBC programme 'On Side'. I wasn't too nervous about being grilled by John Inverdale. I was more concerned about not falling over when I walked on. They have this metal bridge in the studio along which the guests have to walk when they are introduced. At the end of it you have to make a sharp turn to reach your seat. Apparently, under the glare of the lights and with the noise of the applause, one guest went straight on and would have finished up in the audience if he hadn't been pulled back.

It was good to meet the other guests, Paula Radcliffe, Nasser Hussain and Bobby Robson. Things became quite animated when Bobby got into a disagreement with Nasser over cheating in cricket. I thought the show had gone OK but it was only when my parents played back the video of it at home that my mum discovered an awful truth. I did everything right along the metal bridge, turned off to shake hands with Inverdale perfectly but as I went to take my seat, he had to wipe his hands on his trousers – clammy palms.

I did a trailer with Inverdale for 'EastEnders'. It was at the time when Phil Mitchell had been shot and for the trailer the BBC wanted a number of us to guess who'd done it. This was difficult since I don't watch the programme but I managed to get around it by not actually answering the question at any point – a talent developed in rugby interviews.

At the same time as I was attempting to promote myself, I was also doing community work for the club. This side of the Falcons has really taken off which means extra demands on the players, but ones we enjoy. I took the Cup along to my adopted school and went down to Westgate School with Ross Nesdale to coach some youngsters in the basics of the game at the Lloyds–TSB rugby skills roadshow.

Punting mini rugby balls into basketball hoops 40 metres away was a hit with the kids, as was showing off the key rugby skill of throwing a ball up in the air, performing a forward roll and catching it on the way down. Everything was going well until the touch rugby match at the end. I managed to injure my elbow and burn my trousers sliding over on a sportshall floor for a try from 10 metres out – body on the line for the cause, and all that.

Promotional work also entailed going along to local rugby clubs for quiz evenings. The format was three Falcons players against three characters from the hosting club. The rounds included a true or false section. Each individual had three stories read out about them and the opposition had to guess which was the one that really happened. The tales about me included an accusation that I had once won a ballroom dancing competition back in Surrey (false) and one about my driving (true).

When I was 19 and very inexperienced behind the wheel, I drove the wrong way around a roundabout. I saw the traffic heading towards me, realised what I had done and in panic steered towards the safety of the traffic island in the middle. I managed to get the car up on to it but it must have been quite a sight, what with cars slowing down to look at the marooned vehicle parked on the roundabout. I ducked down, pretending I was fiddling with something important inside and banged on the steering wheel as if there was a fault, until the coast was clear and then sped off the right way.

After the quiz there was usually a question and answer session. At Percy Park Rugby Club the teasers we were asked included: 1. Do you want a race outside? 2. My mate has the best sidestep in the world. Do you want to see it? The correct answers were no and yes. The chap who asked this had a stool put out for him to step around and he turned out to be pretty good. The Falcons contract is still in the post; in fact I think it may be lost.

chapter ten

A pain in the neck

Newcastle's spring slump left us needing to regroup. The long Premiership season had reached the run-in and we wanted a big finish. If we won our last three league matches against London Irish, Rotherham and Saracens, and scored a bonus point in each, we would finish fourth. That would give us a home draw in the play-offs and a strong chance of qualifying for the Heineken Cup through the league.

We felt the feat was within our capabilities although it did not look like it when, 30 seconds after kick-off at Kingston Park, Richard Kirke scored a try for Irish. We hit back within two minutes with one of our own – my bi-monthly try – and that set the scene for a points-fest. Apart from my touchdown, which came about when a gap opened up in the Irish defence 10 metres out, we scored another four tries in the first period, with me putting over all six conversions. It was 42–17 at half-time. We allowed them back into the game after the break and ended up clinging on at the end for a 42–35 victory.

The defensive effort at the end keeping out Irish was to have a major effect on the remainder of my season. Going in for a tackle on one of their centres in the last five minutes, I suffered a whiplash injury to my neck. It wasn't as if I was going for a big hit; it was just that I got into the wrong position to make the tackle. The guy cut back inside Tom May, which meant he was my man, and as I lined him up with my right shoulder, he cut back again into my head. Ouch!

I lay on the ground in agony. Searing heat burnt into my neck, across my back and down my left shoulder. No matter where I put myself, the pain would not go away. I recognised the sensation. I had first felt it playing for Hampshire as a 16-year-old when I went in for a tackle and came out with the same sharp pain down my arm. It went away after rest and treatment but there were recurrences. When it happened during my first season with Newcastle with the pain across my front as well as my back, I went for a scan. What it showed was that the diameter of the canal around my spine is very slightly narrower than the average. That means that every now and then, after a succession of blows, the nerves may pinch together. It is not dangerous. In a normal job it would never be a problem, but tackling 16 stone rugby players is not really a normal job. The weakness is part of my make-up and is going to affect me in the game I've chosen to play. But considering I've had the problem for five years, things haven't gone too badly.

I was due to fly down to meet up with the England squad for the French game on the night of the London Irish game and the club felt it would be wise to have an X-ray first to check everything was OK. It revealed no structural damage but this time was slightly different from previous recurrences because there was muscle damage as well as the pain from the nerves.

I realised as much next morning. I had caught my flight to London and spent the night at Pennyhill Park but when I woke up I could hardly move my neck. I hadn't been feeling too bad when I arrived but the injury had stiffened up as I slept. I was concerned that I wouldn't be fit for the weekend but the medical team assured me this was bound to happen and set about sorting me out in time.

I had to sleep in a neck collar and undergo various anti-inflammatory treatments, as well as have regular massages from Richard Wegrzyk, the team masseur. This was when the team hotel came into its own because the physio room was on hand all the time just yards away from my room.

Clive Woodward was in constant contact with the medical men, checking on my progress, but as a precaution Austin Healey trained at fly-half.

Kicking was a definite no-no for me early on in the week as it would have been too painful; but there was nothing I could about it so I didn't fret. I watched training with Kyran Bracken and Richard Hill, who were also nursing injuries. We took the inevitable flak for sitting the sessions out. Our team-mates dragged on imaginary cigars now and again to illustrate what they thought of the smoking jacket and panama set on the sidelines.

For once, the England side had to be rejigged because of injuries. As well as calling up Julian White for Phil Vickery, Clive gave Steve Borthwick the nod as second-row replacement for Danny Grewcock who had broken his jaw playing for Saracens.

England had been lucky over the season. Up to then, we had been able to name virtually an unchanged side. When you play regularly with the same team-mates it stands to reason that the side must benefit. The more time I spent outside Matt Dawson and inside Mike Catt, the more I instinctively knew what they were going to do in certain situations. Chopping and changing means the established players find themselves having to adapt to colleagues who react and do things differently, a process that takes time.

A settled, successful side is also the ideal environment in which to introduce one or two new players. When I was 18 I was fortunate enough to come into a Newcastle side in this position. Jason Robinson enjoyed a similar luxury with England.

Continuity of selection helps but luck does play a part. However much coaches may want to wrap their players in cotton wool, there are times in training when you have to go at it full on, whatever the injury risk. There is only so much benefit that can be gained playing against tackle bags. Eventually you need realistic opposition to disrupt the way you are trying to play so you learn to be ruthless yourself. Live opposition is part of the way we work in training.

We are encouraged to be sensible with injuries, though. There is no point trying to be a hero in practice if it means missing the match by aggravating a niggle. If we're not fit, we don't train – maybe that explains part of our good fortune.

Clive's selections to replace the injured guys, and his decision to recall Phil Greening for Dorian West, were close ones and the players who lost out were obviously not best pleased. They got a chance to take on the ones who had been picked ahead of them during a forwards' session which became heated. While the backs were preparing themselves mentally for the French, the forwards were clearly readying themselves for the physical battle. Forwards are a different breed from the backs. You would struggle to catch us doing this sort of thing but they seemed quite happy with it. I suppose there is a more physical element to everything they do in training so there is more opportunity for sparks to fly. The session was the talk of the dinner table on Monday night. Emotions are vital but as always were left out on the training pitch.

My condition was not much better next morning but, bad neck or not, I had an appointment with royalty. Prince Andrew popped in to say hello to the squad and publicise the NSPCC's Full Stop campaign, of which he was patron. We were all given black NSPCC caps to wear. Mine looked terrible so I passed it on to Joe Worsley, who is known as 'The Swede' because of his seemingly large head, and it looked even worse on him.

The cause is one all the players support. Most of the team, including me, wear the NSPCC's green circle on our England tracksuits before matches.

I wondered how I should address Prince Andrew but we just talked informally so there was no need for titles. We ended up chatting about professionalism and how the game had changed since the amateur era. He seemed to know his rugby.

By Wednesday I felt I was well enough to train so I headed out to Sandhurst with the team. The idea of training at a military base is to use their good facilities but also to take advantage of tight security. There is no danger of an opposition spy infiltrating one of our sessions when the country's finest are guarding the place.

It is hard enough for us to get in sometimes. We are supposed to telephone ahead for clearance to train at Sandhurst but on a couple of occasions I've turned up there with Dave Alred for a kicking session and found the message has not got through. It was fairly obvious who we were in our England gear but there was no question of being waved through. Everything had to be checked and re-checked.

Wednesday was important because it was the last major team-training session of the week. Thursdays are usually free bar a kicking session and we just have an important but light run on Friday mornings. My neck still was not perfect. I could not turn my head around properly and I sometimes found myself having to guess exactly where to pass. We dropped a few balls at the start of the session, which was quite frustrating, but by the end we were ticking over nicely. I was able to kick for the first time in the week.

By Thursday my neck had eased considerably but snow and wind hampered my kicking session. What with the missed days earlier on in the week, Friday's kicking practice at Twickenham was doubly important.

Unfortunately, because of the weather, the groundsman was ultra-keen to keep the pitch covered. Every time I looked up there would be less and less grass visible as the groundstaff moved in with their plastic sheeting. I felt like Indiana Jones with the walls closing in around me. It was not the session I had hoped for.

In the coaches' pre-match analysis, a lot of emphasis was placed on stamping out any complacency in the wake of our recent form and France's home defeat by Wales. They had made six personnel changes and a positional alteration from the side beaten at the Stade de France. Centre Thomas Lombard, lock David Auradou, flanker Christophe Moni and No. 8 Christophe Juillet were all dropped, and they had been hard hit by injuries. Their pre-match camp near Bordeaux had been difficult for them with the sizeable Stade Francais contingent missing their flight and arriving late. France had been disrupted – of that there was no question – but we were all aware they still had the capacity to hit form, turn it on and rip opponents apart. Any team who can beat New Zealand, and beat them well, in a World Cup semi-final and then repeat the dose, as France had done in the autumn, had to be a force to be reckoned with.

They proved it in the first half when they asked us more defensive questions than any other team during the season and went into the interval 16–13 up. The French have so much natural pace and they managed to work Christophe Dominici and Philippe Bernat-Salles into space on the outside, which caused us problems. They had said beforehand this was where they thought our defensive system was vulnerable.

If a team does get around the outside, it is not as damaging as if they break you through the middle. In the first instance, the full-back or opposite wing can still move across to snuff out an attack but in the second you are in big trouble if the ball carrier has supporting team-mates flooding through.

I didn't think our system was at fault as much as our execution. France broke up our defensive pattern partly because we made so many mistakes with the ball, gifting quick possession to them.

After the break, when we kept hold of the ball, things were different. We did not set out to alter our approach radically; it was just we were able to retain the ball through more phases and crack open their defence. In many ways, the match mirrored our Wednesday training session – patchy start, great finish.

There wasn't a huge gap between the two sides until the last quarter when we raced away to run out 48–19 winners. The rush of tries included a deserved one by Mike Catt from an overhead kick by Austin Healey. I was waiting to deliver a more conventional chip when Austin showed us his Leicester party trick. It illustrated the freedom with which we were playing.

I was glad Mike scored – he was my England player of the season. His distribution from inside-centre had been superb all year. It was good to see Matt Perry come on in this period and I helped him score a try, too, but it cost him some ribbing afterwards. I spotted him looking up at the giant video screen to see himself in full flow as he crossed the line, at which point the commentator said, 'He has a look at himself and he likes what he sees.'

Afterwards quite a lot was made of the fitness disparity but I don't think enough emphasis was placed on the fact that they were having to defend for such long periods. It is a different ball game if you are attacking. I compare it to our pre-match warm-up at Newcastle. Steve Black picks out individuals to lead the side on a run around the pitch. If you are setting the pace, you seem to have more energy than if you are chasing. It's the same with attack and defence. If you have the ball, you are on edge, waiting to explode through a gap, but if you are making tackle after tackle the effort eventually takes its toll. The way England kept possession in that second period meant France had to do an awful lot of work.

All in all it was a highly satisfying afternoon for us. It was topped off for me by passing Rob Andrew's English points-scoring record of 396 with a penalty in first-half injury time. I had missed my previous attempt – nothing to do with the record, just a poor kick – but this one from 40 metres was better. Although the press had made a song and dance about it during the week, I had forgotten about the mark and didn't realise I had done it until I heard the announcement on the way to the dressing room at half-time. The only important thing at the time was what the kick did in the context of the game, but it will be nice when I have retired to look back and see my name in the record books.

Just to be mentioned in the same breath as Rob was an honour – he was my hero when I was growing up. I remember watching him kick 12 out of 12 against Canada. It was an awesome display. To overtake his England total is an achievement to be proud of.

Comparing our figures is unfair really because Rob did not start kicking seriously until the latter part of his career. He worked hard with Dave Alred to develop his skill and finished up being the best in the business. When I arrived at Newcastle I used to practise kicking with him and I could have had no better mentor. Now, as director of rugby rather than a player, he is office-bound but often when he sees me practising, he will be tempted down to join in. He is my employer but also a friend.

Rob and Steve Bates have had a huge and varied input into my development as a rugby player. In the first couple of years, they helped me learn to keep my composure and taught me how to put a game plan into operation. In the third year, it was decision-making and dealing mentally with big matches. This year has been different again. They have tried to help me manage the stresses and strains of playing so many games. Both underlined the importance of rest and helped me to help myself. They have been there and done everything I am encountering now, so they are the perfect people to offer advice. Rob was there to say well done after I had broken his record.

After the game, for the first time in a long while, we had a debutant to humiliate. Steve Borthwick had to undergo the traditional ritual of singing a solo on the team bus on the way to the dinner. I remember performing an excruciatingly embarrassing version of Oasis's 'Wonderwall' after my first cap and Borthwick chose another old favourite, 'You've Lost That Loving Feeling'. It was an interesting rendition. He was also supposed to have a drink with each member of the team but I think he escaped quite lightly. I didn't have one with him, anyway.

I've known Steve since England Schools days when he was in the side despite being a year younger than the others. That was quite an achievement for a forward. If he keeps progressing, I'm sure he has a big future ahead of him – not as a singer, though.

It was an odd feeling that evening because with the Ireland game still to play in October, there was unfinished business to attend to in the Six Nations. It would have been better to have played the Ireland game on neutral ground and got it out of the way. There was no sense of climax to the international season.

However, we still had cause to look back on the season with satisfaction. We were unbeaten and the style with which we had played during the Six Nations had been a real testament to the coaching staff. The try dam had eventually burst. The entertaining rugby we had produced was a real plus for the players, too. I spend a lot of time practising my skills so it is only natural that I want to use them in matches. Many records fell to us along the way but what was especially rewarding was when something we practised worked well during a game. That's when all those hours of work seem worth it.

People put us on a pedestal after our performances, saying we had finally broken the southern-hemisphere monopoly at the top of the world game and that we were one of the top two sides around. I know we can't say that until we have beaten these sides consistently – and away from home. That is the next major challenge we face.

We can get better. Most of this team will hopefully be around when we arrive at the 2003 World Cup and there is a good system in place to replace those who won't. Alex Sanderson, another England Schoolboy friend of mine, spent the week before the France game with the squad to get accustomed to life with England so that when his time comes, as it surely will, he will be ready. Other players, including Jamie Noon, did the same during the season.

The Premiership is developing the right calibre of player and England are bringing on that talent wisely. We have no right to expect to win anything. Success will only come through hard work – but the future could look good.

If the season was arranged properly, we could become even better. Three days after the French game, Newcastle had to visit bottom of the table Rotherham in the Premiership. It was ludicrous. I wasn't in any fit state to play. My body felt beaten up. I had taken another bang on the neck during the French game and my groin was beginning to ache again. The pain was spreading into my lower back, too. The relentless pressure of kicking virtually six days a week for the past eight months was taking its toll.

As the injuries accumulated and the weather warmed up, a kind of lethargy came over me. Hauling myself out of bed for training became increasingly difficult. Perhaps it was my body's way of telling anyone who would listen that the season was too long.

Dave Walder was injured for the Rotherham game, too, so Tom May had a rare outing at fly-half.

Anyone who thought the relegated Yorkshiremen would be a soft touch at Clifton Lane was in for a nasty shock. We allowed them to build up a substantial lead before hauling them back to win in a hectic finish. The five points we gained meant we still had a chance of fourth place. The task was to beat Saracens on Easter Sunday and hope Bristol turned over Northampton the following day. We had to raise ourselves for one last, big effort.

I asked to be wheeled out to play and, just as at Rotherham, we allowed Sarries to build up an early lead. We launched our usual big finish to bring them within touching distance but in the last move of the game Gary Armstrong fought his way over the line to score what would have been the winning try, only to be held up trying to touch down. We had fallen short and Rob was not amused. He accused Sarries of employing time-wasting tactics to run the clock down. The odd tactical cramp attack is part and parcel of the professional game but it was frustrating from our point of view to be slowed down by another 'injury' as we tried to put some pace into the game.

Rob endured a bad day all round after being told off by the touch judge for straying out of his coaching area. He made a point of tip-toeing very deliberately back into the corner of his box, a distance of about a foot, before carrying on as he left off, much to the crowd's amusement.

It wasn't such a great day for me, either. I had to go off when my neck became too much of a problem. I took three big hits in the wrong area, one of which was caused by my own man when Inga knocked Tim Horan into me. I was still staggering around when Saracens moved the ball to the side of a ruck and the line opened up for Richard Hill. I went into position to stop him but he ran straight at me so I had no choice but to go for the tackle. I flew into him as hard as I could and tried to hold him up as we went to ground. I thought I had done it but stretching back in the tackle brought on the agonising pain again and I had to let go. My efforts had bought Newcastle time and Ian Peel managed to get his hands under the ball to prevent the try. However, I was finished. My league season ended being escorted from the pitch as Newcastle went down to a defeat that meant a sixth-place finish.

I felt we had under-achieved, even though we had won as many games as we had lost. We had let too many matches get away. Consistency was the key and we hadn't found it. Recurring themes had been slow starts and failures to close out games. Both probably pointed to mental weaknesses. Often we would play well, establish a lead and then subconsciously relax when we had built up a cushion. It was a bad trait. It wasn't as if we faded because of lack of fitness – we were one of the best-prepared sides around as our sprint finish in the

Cup final proved – but mentally we weren't always where we needed to be.

One thing was for sure – we would emerge a better side for the experience. A lot of us young players had grown up together in that punishing Premiership campaign. Our time would come – I was sure of it.

chapter eleven

Adventures in Europe

The introduction of European club competition is one of the best things to happen to rugby union since it went professional. Crossing frontiers to play different opposition provides the challenge English teams need to extend their knowledge and improve. The Heineken Cup has been an undoubted hit, attracting media attention, live television coverage and generally capturing people's imagination.

However, at Newcastle we had to make do with a place in the second-tier European Shield, rugby's equivalent of a news blackout zone. Even though plenty of star players were involved in the tournament, it barely merited a few paragraphs in most papers. There were some fine teams involved in the Shield yet the tournament was unable to attract a sponsor or television coverage until the semi-final stage. That was a shame because, just like the Heineken Cup, it was great experience for the players. The matches had a different feel because they involved new teams and venues.

We attached a high priority to the tournament because we saw it as yet another route into the following season's Heineken Cup. The winners qualified automatically and we thought we had a good chance.

The format was bizarre. The pool matches were played in two clumps, the first in October and the second in January. The quarter-finals followed immediately but then there was a hard-to-fathom two-month gap before the semi-finals. Any momentum that had been built up was allowed to disappear. Like the Six Nations, it might be better to play European rugby in one block in consecutive weeks. That way the players and fans can lock on to each particular tournament more easily.

We had to make do with what was in front of us, though, and that turned out to be an extremely tough group. Treviso, Begles-Bordeaux and Cross Keys represented difficult challenges and we could not have had a worse start. We went to Treviso and lost.

We should have guessed we were heading for a fall during the build-up. Andrew Mower dropped out before we even left for Italy because of a calf injury sustained wrestling Epi Taione. We arrived the day before the game and the players went off to see Venice's wonderful sights. Unfortunately, some of us got lost and ended up seeing too much of them. I find it better to relax the day before a game than walk around and around trying to find where it was I set off from in the first place.

Matters did not improve the next day when we arrived at the ground. There was only one toilet in our small dressing room. It had no door and it was one of the hole-in-the-floor variety – not a great place to achieve calm before the game.

The match itself was a good one and Treviso, particularly their big forwards, played very well. They deserved their win and looked as good, if not better, than Roma and L'Aquila who had qualified for the Heineken Cup.

For me, the consolation in defeat was my first – and best – try of the season, diving swallow-like into the corner after a superb handling move in which Jim Jenner and Epi had important roles. When Epi gave me the ball, I had 25 metres to go on the outside to the try-line

– not usually my forte. But I found some pace from somewhere and made it.

Nevertheless, the loss meant we could not afford another slip if we were to qualify for the quarter-finals. Only the group winners went through and Treviso looked a good enough side not to be beaten by anyone else.

Cross Keys at home proved a different proposition. I was rested for the game but by half-time Newcastle were 75–3 up. The Welsh side played better in the second half and kept us under the 100 mark by a point. It was a good chance for a lot of players to get on the scoresheet, not least Liam Botham who finished with a hat-trick of tries.

I was back in the side for the trip to Bordeaux. That was a great experience with warm sun on our backs in October and a tough game against a good French side, which we won 26–18.

I had a taste of what Newcastle's opponents 'enjoy' during the game when I was rucked by Richard Arnold. He was so eager to get to the ball that it didn't matter who was in the way. I needed some pain-killing ice spray on my shin afterwards. Overall, it was a top day. There was a big crowd and a lively atmosphere and the whole occasion summed up everything European rugby should be about. And then there was Bordeaux to enjoy.

I had been excused England training on the Monday so I was able to join the boys for a rare night out on the town. It was a good chance to let our hair down and although I don't remember all the details about it, I do vaguely recall being involved in a peanut fight in a bar. I'm glad I wasn't around when Gareth Maclure was stripped naked in McDonald's, or when Hugh Vyvyan and Jim Jenner were thrown out of a jazz club. They were mimicking 'The Fast Show' jazz club sketches and the punters, who may not have seen the TV programme, weren't too impressed.

It is pretty rare to have the chance of a night out after an away game in the Premiership because of the long journey back to Newcastle, so we made the most of this one. The management turned a shrewd blind eye. Some of them were sampling plenty of the local wine back at base.

The tournament was structured so we played Bordeaux in back-to-back games, which at least gave us some up-to-date reconnaissance on them for the return at Kingston Park the following week. Obtaining videos of European opponents is a lot harder than with Premiership rivals so there is more thinking on your feet to do on matchday. That can be a good thing.

We were blessed with some typical Newcastle weather to welcome the French – rain and wind – and ran out fairly convincing winners. I was on the bench but I still had the dubious pleasure of being picked out by the drug testers afterwards. There were no worries over the result but delivering the sample was a concern. As soon as your number is picked out, the tester keeps an eye on you until you produce a urine specimen for him. The dehydration that follows a game and the unfamiliar position of someone looking over your shoulder at the urinal can make it difficult.

My heart sank when I was summoned because I had a flight to catch from Teesside Airport that night for England training the next day. All the Newcastle flights had been full so I had been booked on to the 6.25, which did not leave much time. A drugs test was the last thing I needed. Fortunately, I came up trumps with the sample and made the flight.

The elastic nature of the European Shield season meant a long wait for our next match – the crucial return tie with Treviso. After studying the tournament rules, our boffins worked out that we had to beat them by two clear tries or by one try and 14 points to go ahead of them at the top of the group. If two teams were level on wins, the placings would be determined by the aggregate number of tries, then points, in the two matches the sides had played against each other.

Treviso had scored two tries to our one in Italy, and beaten us by 13 points.

Having to win by a specific margin put some pressure on us. All our decisions during the match were made with this in mind and we had to be prepared to sacrifice penalties in the search for tries. We managed one by half-time through Micky Ward after a lineout drive, and although we had to be patient, the important second came with 17 minutes left. I threw a long pass out to Inga and he beat a few men to score. George Graham's try five minutes later gave us some breathing space. Treviso came back with a late try of their own to cut our victory margin to 11 points but we knew we were through.

The Italians thought differently, though, and despite the fact that the rules, as we understood them, were clear, their insistence that they had gone through on points difference began to create doubts in our minds. With no European Shield officials on hand Dave Thompson, our owner, was in a flap; he even sided with Treviso at one point. However, much to our relief, confirmation eventually came through that we had been right all along.

The outcome was vital because it meant all we had to do was to triumph at Cross Keys in our final group game to qualify. Victory would carry with it the added bonus of a home quarter-final draw. That advantage went to the four pool winners with the best records.

After our 99–8 win at home over Cross Keys, a lot of people thought the away game, for which I was rested, would be a walk in the park. In one sense it was. Their first XV pitch was unplayable because it was half-flooded and half-frozen. The options were to stay an extra night in Cross Keys and wait to see if it improved, or play in a local park. The boys did not fancy the first option so we were left with the park pitch. Their chairman told Rob not to worry because he had sent the first XV to clear the sheep off it and the second XV to clear the droppings away.

It was like playing schools rugby again. The likes of Va'aiga Tuigamala and Gary Armstrong had to change on the touchlines; the grandstand was in reality a bandstand and the press bench was a park bench. At regular intervals, the touch judge had to push the crowd back off the pitch.

Newcastle overcame everything to win 25–11 but the bus driver refused to let the team on to the bus at the end because of all the mud so they had to trudge back to the Cross Keys clubhouse for a cold shower – priceless. Shame I missed that one.

The bizarre victory in Wales earned us a home quarter-final against Mont-de-Marsan from south-west France who had emerged out of Bristol's group. They would ordinarily have been able to call on the services of Fijian sevens king Waisale Serevi and Test centre Viliame Satala. However, Serevi was injured and Satala was serving a ban, which made our task easier.

They were up for it, though. Their flanker, Philippe Alaoui, seemed to be on a mission and he got himself sent off by referee Clayton Thomas inside 20 minutes for throwing a haymaker.

Playing against 14 men gave us the freedom to produce fast, flowing rugby and we cruised through 61–23. It was an assist day for me. I gave four scoring passes but nobody returned the favour.

We awaited the semi-final draw with interest. We didn't particularly want an away trip to either of the two French survivors, Agen and Narbonne, but on the other hand we knew how evenly matched we were with Harlequins after our three meetings during the season. Fate decreed a 22 April re-match with Quins, at Headingley rather than Twickenham. There was a lot riding on it.

The build-up to the game was surrounded in controversy when the threat of uncontested scrums reared its head. Harlequins failed to register a reserve hooker after Keith Wood popped a rib cartilage so it left open the possibility that if Tani Fuga could not complete the match, pushing would be outlawed. We had no objection to Quins adding another specialist hooker to their list but European Rugby Cup stood firm on the issue.

In my view, it would not have been asking too much of a prop to play there. While health and safety issues have to be paramount, particularly in the front row, I'm sure the adrenaline of the occasion would have carried along whoever stepped in. As it turned out, Fuga stayed on for the full 80 minutes despite doubts over his ankle, and had a great game.

Craig Chalmers came in for the injured Paul Burke and scored all Quins' points in a narrow win, which gave them some measure of revenge for the Tetley's Bitter Cup final.

Quins built their victory on a very good defensive performance but one which bordered on the edge of the law all afternoon. They told us openly afterwards their plan had been to stop us playing by slowing down and occasionally killing the ball. They got away with it and did it well. It's OK doing that for a one-off encounter but a team cannot do it all season. Opponents will find their way around it with better ball presentation than we managed.

Quins had been playing well since Christmas and they were more than chuffed to reach the final. Apparently, some of the players had already booked their holidays after failing to reach the championship play-offs.

The game spelt a disappointing end to my domestic season. The neck injury that had been troubling me for some time flared up again. Having received the all clear on Friday after a scan, I felt as good going into the match as I had before the England versus France match. However, I took an accidental but heavy knee to the head from Harlequins full-back Ryan O'Neill in the opening 10 minutes and that set it off again. With hindsight, I suppose I might have been wiser to go off at that point. I went down again in the 50th minute when the jarring caused by Will Greenwood's tackle caused me more pain and I finally had to go off in the last minute after it happened twice more. I did not want to – we were only 17–12 down and I thought we could pull off another Twickenham – but the medical staff insisted I left the field. I was in a lot of pain. So, momentarily, was Gary Armstrong when George Graham tried to help him recover from a knock by squirting Lucozade into his eyes instead of water.

The defeat meant we had to wait to see whether our Cup win was enough to carry us into the Heineken Cup. What it all boiled down to were the quarter-finals of the championship play-offs. If the home sides won, we were safe whether we beat Bath in our tie or not. I was pretty confident it would work out in our favour. Leicester, Northampton and Wasps are all formidable at home but I did have a slight concern that Sarries might turn Northampton over. In the end, Saints won easily, as did Leicester against London Irish, and with us going down at Bath, it was left to Wasps to see us through by beating Gloucester. After a season of toil, we had to sit helplessly by and cross our fingers. It was a close-run thing but they did it.

I decided to ignore the game until it was over. There was nothing I could do to affect the outcome and following its progress would have been just as exhausting as playing in it. So I was slumped in front of the television at home when I heard the news from Mark. A text message from the club confirmed we had made it. I felt a massive sense of relief. After being denied the chance when we won the league three seasons earlier and narrowly missing out the following year, qualifying for the Heineken Cup capped an up-and-down season with an undeniable high. We had achieved what we had set out to do. Europe would be a massive stage on which to compete the following season.

We would be welcoming back Pat Lam whom I was excited about playing alongside. He made a monster contribution to the championship-winning side and is a player who can lift those around him, as he proved again when Northampton won the Heineken Cup.

However, we were going to have to survive without Ross Nesdale, our Kiwi hooker, who had been at Newcastle since the game went professional. He was heading back to New Zealand with his wife Jo. Ross was an outstanding player and one of the main reasons why Newcastle had such a good lineout and set-piece. He had a massive influence on the team. He had another side to him, too. On our big night out in Bordeaux, he was found on his own in a bar arm-wrestling locals for drinks. Ross's farewell was so low-key that I never had a chance to thank one of the foundation stones of Newcastle's success. On top of that, he had been a friendly face to a shy 18-year-old. He popped along one day to training to say he was off. The implications didn't really register until I asked him if he'd be along again to Newcastle soon. 'In a few years,' he said.

Dave Walder, Jamie Noon and Michael Stephenson's inclusion in the England squad to tour the USA and Canada was just reward for their immense efforts and performances. Tom May was crowned the Newcastle player of the season, which was some consolation after just missing out on a tour place.

It had been quite a season for all concerned and we signed off spectacularly around the city on Mad Monday. The previous year I had missed the fleet of white limos we had hired to take us to the races and then on a pub crawl around Newcastle at our end-of-season celebration. This time I skipped the afternoon session, which used up our fines money, and joined the rest of the squad with Gareth Maclure once the drinking was well underway. We took the predictable abuse for being lightweights.

Everyone headed off into Newcastle city centre for a night of revelry. It was high-spirited and harmless, although one unnamed member of the side was given a friendly shoeing when he fell down on the bar floor under the influence. He dishes enough out so he deserved it.

The night got very silly. I started off a stupid hand-shaking game with complete strangers. One unsuspecting punter found himself gripped in a series of unusual positions in a virtuoso display of hand gymnastics. He looked at me in a way that suggested I was scaring him. This performance set the early pace, but I found myself overtaken by props Ian Peel and Micky Ward. Faced with the heavies, people were less inclined to withdraw their hands and found themselves on the receiving end. Peely set the record with 15 different positions, including a cheek pinch.

One poor friend of our reserve hooker, Billy Balshen, walked straight into a four-man assault when he was introduced to us. He was exposed to an aggregate of 50 'hand-shakes', although the precise definition was stretched by nose pinching and playful punches.

The squad moved on to a nightclub called the Sea Club in town, but it shut far too early for my liking. Because I go out so rarely, I tend to make the most of it when it happens. My brother and I put the word around that there was a party afterwards at Michael Stephenson's house. He didn't know about it until he arrived back in a taxi to find a queue of friends, team-mates and complete strangers outside.

We are notorious for this sort of thing. We set up a party, have a great time, and disappear back to our house. As this one was dying down, we put the word around that there was another party at Pete Massey's about to start but by then everyone was running out of steam. A long and enjoyable night ended with a taxi back and I crawled into bed. Ahead of me was an important month's preparation, the greatest challenge of my career was on the horizon. The Lions.

chapter twelve

Australia-bound

I learnt of my Lions selection via my dad. The make-up of the party had been kept a closely guarded secret until the morning of the announcement when the management had rung around the players. I was on a flight down from Newcastle to London at the time so they couldn't get hold of me and by the time I arrived at Heathrow, the cat was out of the bag. Dad was able to break the news. He was very proud.

Even though my name had been included in the initial 67-man party and the season had gone well, I never took anything for granted and was delighted when I found out for sure. The Lions are the pinnacle of a northern-hemisphere player's career and to make the trip was fantastic. I had a video of the 1989 Lions tour to Australia at home and to think I would be retracing the steps of Finlay Calder's party was exhilarating.

In all, there were 18 Englishmen, 10 Welshmen, six Irishmen and three Scots included in the squad:

Full-backs: Iain Balshaw (England), Matt Perry (England).

Wings: Dan Luger (England), Jason Robinson (England), Ben Cohen (England), Dafydd James (Wales).

Centres: Brian O'Driscoll (Ireland), Mike Catt (England), Will Greenwood (England), Rob Henderson (Ireland), Mark Taylor (Wales).

Stand-offs: Jonny Wilkinson (England), Neil Jenkins (Wales), Ronan O'Gara (Ireland).

Scrum-halves: Robert Howley (Wales), Matt Dawson (England), Austin Healey (England).

Props: Tom Smith (Scotland), Darren Morris (Wales), Dai Young (Wales), Jason Leonard (England), Phil Vickery (England).

Hookers: Keith Wood (Ireland), Phil Greening (England), Robin McBryde (Wales).

Second rows: Scott Murray (Scotland), Martin Johnson (England, captain), Danny Grewcock (England), Malcolm O'Kelly (Ireland), Jeremy Davidson (Ireland).

Back row: Richard Hill (England), Neil Back (England), Lawrence Dallaglio (England), Colin Charvis (Wales), Martyn Williams (Wales), Scott Quinnell (Wales), Simon Taylor (Scotland).

The management team was: manager Donal Lenihan (Ireland); coach Graham Henry (Wales); assistant coach Andy Robinson (England); defence Phil Larder (England); kicking Dave Alred (England); video analysis Alun Carter (Wales); conditioning Steve Black (Geordie); doctor James Robson (Scotland); physio Mark Davies (Wales); masseur Richard Wegrzyk (England); baggage man Pat O'Keefe (Ireland); administrative secretary Joan Moore (Ireland); media manager Alex Broun (Australia).

I was sure the make-up of the party would work well. There had been another fairly large English contingent in 1997 and the Lions had enjoyed a fabulously successful tour of South Africa.

There was a month to kill between Newcastle's last game and the Lions' departure and my main priority was to get my neck right for the trip. I also needed to recharge my batteries after the exertions of the domestic season, but I kept myself in shape, too. In fact, I probably did too much on the hard grounds because my groin started giving me trouble. It was not the side that had been operated on, and the ache was worryingly familiar.

It was not helped by all the kicking practice I was doing. I was mad keen to familiarise myself with the rugby ball we would be using in Australia, which has a different weight and texture from the one we use in the UK. It's similar to the one the Italians use. I was determined that by the time I was kicking the thing in matches, any mental hang-ups would be left in England. I don't think I ever quite mastered it. Kicking would go well for several days and then, inexplicably, it would fall apart. The inconsistency was maddening.

With time on my hands for once, I was able to play some golf, throw a frisbee or an American football around the neighbours' land with Sparks and go along to see the latest venture in the Wilkinson household's sporting season. It was my brother's debut for Gateshead Thunder rugby league team in the Northern Ford Premiership. Having been swallowed up by Hull in a merger the previous season, the Thunder had re-formed at semi-pro level. Their record up to this point – played 19, lost 19 – did not show the full story. They had turned to Sparks after the end of his Falcons conditioning commitments.

I went along to Swinton to support and was pleased to see him come through his first game unscathed. However, despite a plucky performance from their new rangy recruit, Gateshead lost again, 20–8. I also joined the Thunder travelling fans at Widnes and Hunslet where they picked up that elusive first win. I was proud to be there to see it and they won the following week as well. Sparks, who played at centre and loose forward, was unable to finish the season as he headed out to

Australia to do some conditioning work with the New South Wales State of Origin side, and the Sydney City league team.

My commitments to Newcastle continued during the summer with promotional duties including an enjoyable morning opening a new youth club in Newbiggin. The Falcons' hefty prop Marius Hurter and I were invited along to accompany Ant and Dec in cutting the ribbon in front of 150 kids. We were definitely the support act. Ant and Dec are local boys made good and when they were introduced the place almost needed repairing straightaway. The noise nearly took the roof off. When the time came to sign autographs, I was nearly knocked down in the stampede to get to them. Surplus to requirements, I almost resorted to signing the backs of kids' shirts while they queued.

Ant and Dec were good value – brilliant in a question-and-answer session and interested in the rugby. They knew all about my neck injury. In fact, everybody did. It seemed to be one of the talking points ahead of our departure.

While I was confident rest would put me in good shape, I did go along to a specialist for some Frankenstein-type treatment. That wasn't its medical name but what else can you call passing electric impulses through your body? The idea was to check where any weaknesses might be and therefore pinpoint where the nerve was being aggravated.

The results did not tell me much I did not already know but, importantly, they reassured me that there was nothing fundamentally wrong. By the time the Lions met up I was nearly there. I was still advised by Steve Black not to risk any contact work, which was highly frustrating but hugely important. I was desperate to gain people's confidence and respect by training hard. The fact that I couldn't do so left me feeling like a spare part.

We congregated at Tylney Hall in Hampshire on Saturday, 26 May where we stayed for a week before setting off for Australia. The management deliberately chose somewhere none of the players knew so we would all be in the same boat. The week was critical to our development as a squad.

I was a little apprehensive, heading into the unknown. With Newcastle and England we tend to stay in the same places and follow the same schedule each time, and that familiarity acts as a kind of support. Here, we were taken out of that comfort zone. However, it was an exciting prospect meeting up with players I did not really know. We were spread around by the management to stop any cliques developing, but most of the players took it upon themselves to mix outside their normal circles anyway. This was one of the most enjoyable parts of a successful week.

I shared a room with Dafydd James, or Jammo as the Welsh boys know him. I had met him once before. He is a very nice bloke but he was a bit perplexed by my habit of losing the room key, which I did about 20 times. He is a worrier, a bit like me I suppose. He was always concerned about being late or whether he had the right kit with him or what we might be doing in training. Dafydd is also quite tidy so he wasn't too impressed at tripping over my stuff, which was littered all over the floor, on the way to the toilet at night. He isn't in the Neil Back class, though. When I was sharing with Backy later in the tour, I would throw rolled-up paper at the bin, miss, and he would be there in a flash to pick it up for me.

Tidiness was a virtue because we had so much stuff. We were each supplied with four bags of adidas training kit and Eden Park civvies. I spent a lot of time trying it all on but I couldn't find any Lions match kit. That, as we were to learn, was too precious to hand out at this stage.

After the light-hearted greetings and first day at school excitement came a sobering talk by Syd Millar. Syd was a Lion in his propping days and he went on to coach the wonderfully successful 1974 vintage as well as managing the 1980 squad, so he was the ideal man to put across the ethos of being a Lion. He outlined the honour we had been given and the responsibility we all held as keepers of the flame, and how much we would have to put in to the trip. Prepare yourselves, he said, this is going to be a hard, hard few weeks. His words were followed by a talk from our manager Donal Lenihan and coach Graham Henry.

I had met Graham just once before, so, as far as I was concerned, I was starting from scratch with him. I didn't know how he coached or how he interacted. He didn't open the book too far in that first talk, which was essentially some preparatory comments about training. But he did offer a glimpse of a fierce ambition. There was one aim to this tour, he stressed, and that was to win every game.

That evening we had our first session with Impact, the company in charge of moulding us together on our acclimatisation week. Having seen 'Living with Lions', the video of the 1997 tour to South Africa, I had some idea of what lay ahead.

We were put into challenging environments and asked to carry out unfamiliar tasks. The common theme was dependence on others. Trust is a prerequisite of being a successful side and the tasks were a way of earning that trust before we had to put our faith in each other on the field.

The tasks were varied and began with logistical exercises. Part of one involved dividing into teams of nine and trying to find a way of fitting them all inside a small hula hoop. As everyone was carefully trying to squeeze in, Blackie hoisted me up on to his shoulders and charged in to the hoop, deliberately barging every other person out in the process. He then innocently inquired, 'Everybody in?' Nothing brings people together better than laughter and from up high the view of scattered Lions was particularly amusing.

Then there was a physical challenge. It involved racing dragon boats in teams of 12. I was the stroke at the front of our boat, setting the pace for the others. We were always up against it because our team was eccentrically managed. Our instructor took us for cross-country runs between races so we were knackered when it came to the contests themselves.

The instructor, who wasn't part of the Impact team, kept having a go at me for not rowing quickly enough after our exertions. My groin was aching, I was wound up and I spat out my dummy. I let him have a sarcastic barrage, which my team-mates in the boat greeted with a parade of imaginary handbags and laughter. I took plenty of abuse – 'Ooh, you're so aggressive Jonny' that sort of thing – but I wasn't too bothered. I don't lose my rag very often but at least it gave the lads something to talk about. The instructor told us we were useless afterwards and that he hoped we would be better on the rugby field in Australia. As long as he wasn't delivering the team talks, we had a decent chance.

Next day there was a musical task, involving the ordeal of playing in a giant Samba band. The management, backs and forwards were trained separately by professional musicians before coming together to give a performance. The idea was to have 50 hearts beating as one; that meant 50 people playing in time. I am hopeless musically so I thought I made a pretty brave fist of it. The others were even worse.

The backs learnt all the signals very quickly before initiating our own call of 'freestyle' when our instructor was not watching. When Austin Healey gave the signal – a highly sexual thrusting motion – we all smashed the hell out of the instruments and ran around like lunatics. The instructor didn't seem to notice the difference, which suggested that we weren't much cop in the first place.

During our team performance we all had a solo opportunity. When my big moment came, Jason Leonard tried to put his drumstick somewhere it should not go and I lost the beat.

Other, more frightening, Impact sessions followed. I'm apprehensive about heights and the massive network of ropes called Jacob's Ladder that we had to conquer was particularly challenging, as it involved clambering about 40 feet off the ground. The telegraph pole was similarly worrying. The idea was to climb up and balance on the top with one of your team-mates – in my case Richard Hill – and then jump off to catch a trapeze. We had safety harnesses on which was just as well as I fell off and dragged Hilly down with me. So much for teamwork.

There were also less stressful team-building exercises to perform. We divided up into groups and chatted about what would make a successful tour. Gaining each other's respect, winning and ending up as friends at the end of it was a summary of what we decided our aims should be.

For that to happen we had to get to know each other on an individual level. To help with this process we were each presented with an imitation shield, divided into quarters, and asked to fill the sections with details about ourselves. In one quarter we had to spell out what we were like at our best. I put confident, relaxed, ambitious, hard-working, focused, very motivated, playing well and enjoying life. In the next one we had to write down what we were like at our worst – uptight, depressed, stressed, reclusive, lacking motivation and not playing to my expectations. The third quarter was for details of what was important to us. For me that was family, peace of mind, setting ambitious goals and achieving them and not letting down people close to me. Finally we had to say what ticked us off. I wrote down arrogance, playing badly, letting people down and people letting me down. Asked to give a motto to complete the shield, I came up with 'you get out what you put in'. Nice . . .

When we had all finished, the shields were put up on the wall. They made for interesting reading. It was fascinating to see how similar a lot of the answers were. I suppose as professional sportsmen we are driven by similar things.

Tom Smith's was quite revealing. He is a fairly quiet bloke but his shield spelt out that he wasn't unapproachable and he wanted to be included during the tour. I chatted with him on several occasions and found him to be a great guy. Keith Wood shared with him a lot and he finds Tom hilarious company. His rugby isn't bad, either. The handling skills and athletic abilities he has for a front five forward are unbelievable.

To ensure the smooth running of the tour, the players set up several committees. A key figure in the in-house entertainment committee was Brian O'Driscoll. It was his job to drag around the team CD player. He managed to lose CDs wherever we went and by the end of the tour all that remained were the Jam and 'The Best of Neil Diamond'.

Neil Back, a classy dresser, headed the clothing committee while the out-of-house entertainment committee featured Dafydd. He was specifically chosen because people knew the inevitable stick would get to him and he took lots of it when his committee arranged a particularly poor Chinese meal.

There was also a senior players' committee to help direct the tour and I was surprised to find myself co-opted onto it with Martin Johnson, Dai Young, Keith Wood, Lawrence Dallaglio and Rob Howley. I think I was there to represent the younger end.

Along with the planning and the team-building exercises came rugby sessions, which made for long days. We were trying to sort out our moves as early as we could and establish a structure to use throughout the tour. The sore groin stopped me training and while I was getting treatment from Mark Davies, some photographers snapped me. Their angle allowed them to see right into the groin area. I imagine it was like being a sun-bathing film star picked off by the paparazzi.

Before we left we had to fit in a press day with lots of photos and interviews followed by a farewell dinner in the evening with the sponsors. One of the staff was confused by it all and kept telling Mark Taylor, Dafydd James, Robin McBryde and me to take our seats because 'the Lions are coming through soon'.

Next day I popped home to my parents' for an afternoon barbecue and then I was off on a new, exciting and exhausting journey.

On the way to the airport a famous England ritual was re-enacted when Danny Grewcock's passport was stolen and passed around. The sniggers around the bus suggested the joke translated well. Anyone who has ever seen Wolfie, the Tooting revolutionary in the TV programme 'Citizen Smith', will know what we were laughing at when we saw his old picture.

One massive boost for the squad as we took our seats on the plane was the sight of Lawrence Dallaglio. He was such an influential figure that if he had missed the trip because of the knee injury he suffered in the championship play-offs, it would have been a real blow. He knew he would not be able to make the first game against Western Australia but he was such a pivotal figure in 1997, the management were keen to give him extra time to recover. Lawrence was my first room-mate in Australia.

After a seemingly endless flight during which I had a long chat with Neil Jenkins – it was going to be a hard trip for him because he was leaving behind his 18-month-old daughter – we touched down in Perth. Our first base was in Fremantle and when we finally arrived most of the lads went for a run. My groin injury meant a pool session for me but it helped to get the flight out of my system. Our plan was to try to adapt to Australian time quickly by staying up as long as possible.

Lawrence and I had been assigned the cripples room. I didn't see much of him while we were there because he was always out doing his rehab work. He was on a four-week plan to be fit for the Tests and he was very optimistic. He did return quickly on one occasion, though. We were all encouraged to leave our rooms unlocked so other members of the party could pop in for a chat whenever they wanted. This policy almost backfired when a couple of girls appeared with profit on their minds. Smiley Kylie and friend propositioned my roomie by the lift – he politely excused himself and came back to the sanctuary of our room, giving them plenty of time to go away.

We were pestered by one confident young lad who strode into our hotel reception, saw us sitting around and greeted us with, 'G'day, Poms', followed by more anti-British remarks. He decided he wanted our autographs but the lads present weren't too impressed and when he got home he will have been surprised to find the signatures of Elvis Presley, Mickey Mouse and Evel Knievel.

Generally, Fremantle was the perfect place to prepare because it was so low key, rugby wise. Western Australia is Aussie Rules country and we were training at the local club, the Fremantle Dockers. It was a highly professional, impressive set-up with great gym and swimming facilities.

I like watching the game on TV – there's lots of kicking so I'm bound to – and I spend ages kicking an Aussie Rules ball around at home so I was interested to see it first hand. Unfortunately, I wasn't able to do so because of time constraints although I did manage to pick up a Dockers vest while I was there.

The boys were training twice a day, a policy that was to continue for a few weeks, and it was hard graft. The management knew we had to train hard to make the most of the time to prepare, which at the end of a long season back home was tough. The idea was to work us hard at the start of the tour and then taper off by the time the Tests arrived. Lions tours of the past had been 30-game marathons but with just 12 matches on this trip we had no time to lose if we wanted to get things right.

Some players were a bit taken aback but to me it was merely an extension of the way I train anyway. I tend to go over the top on my own so having coaches fill the day did not cause me great stress. After a few weeks off from a team environment, I was going at it fresh and looking forward to some rugby coaching.

It soon became clear that the way the Lions played was going to have to be more intensely structured than the way England play. England's fluid style has developed over several years. The players are getting ever more familiar with each other and we tend to know where we will be on the field most of the time. With the Lions, there simply weren't enough hours in the day to develop this understanding, so Graham Henry, Andy Robinson and the other coaches had to do more pre-planning, sometimes several phases ahead.

While we were becoming accustomed to this, the non-English contingent also found it hard adapting to Phil Larder's defensive system. He had taken sessions with some of them before the tour to get them used to the way he does things, but it tended to be the lads from the other countries who were singled out in early tour training. It was nothing to do with ability, just the fact that they hadn't practised as much as we had.

Perth is meant to be a beautiful city but all we had a chance to see was the zoo with Will Greenwood and Richard Hill. Sky organised a trip there on a rare afternoon off. The highlight was probably a rhino farting in my ear when I was doing an interview but I was also able to feed some wallabies – quite harmless creatures by the look of things, unlike their namesakes.

It turned into a bit of a media event, like other occasions on the tour. The sponsors, ntl, were filming behind the scenes, which was rather awkward, especially at the start. The camera was everywhere – in team meetings, in the dressing room at half-time – and it was quite off-putting. I was as fascinated as anyone else by the footage from the 1997 Lions tour – particularly the intensity in the dressing room – but it is very difficult to be yourself in that situation. When I should have been concentrating on what people were saying I found myself looking for the camera. By the end of the tour I had just about got used to its all-seeing eye.

We were all given cameras of our own to record video diaries but I left mine at home. I didn't want to bore the audience.

Neil Jenkins, who was struggling with a knee problem that affected him all tour, picked up the first training injury of the trip when he collided with Jeremy Davidson. His cut eye needed six stitches. I suppose outsiders must have thought I was secretly chuffed. He and Ronan O'Gara were my rivals for the No. 10 jersey, but it wasn't like that at all. We were all part of the same team so when they were playing I wanted them to do well. I just had to do better, that was all.

The kickers struck up a great relationship even though Ronan kept being called Ryan, Rowan and Roger by Dave Alred. I was used to working one on one or alone so having company was different. We didn't trip over each other because we all worked at our own pace. There was a lot of peer-group support with encouragement whenever any of us hit a particularly good one. It sometimes got quite noisy, which could sound slightly American. In fact, the group feeling brought out the positive in us rather than the negative, which I tend to suffer from.

I was making a gentle reintroduction to kicking at this stage but, frustratingly, I still had to avoid contact work. At least I had some company with Neil and Mike Catt, who had a calf strain. My first real blast came on the morning of the first game, against Western Australia. The guys who weren't involved took part in what was supposed to be a half-contact defensive drill. As is sometimes the case, people got carried away and it ended up being something closer to 80 per cent. For me, that was perfect. I really enjoyed it and my neck came through with no problems. It was a great boost for my confidence.

When the team was announced for Western Australia, there had been one big surprise. Brian O'Driscoll was named at full-back. Why, I don't think he or the rest of us ever found out. He had burst on to the scene as a fantastic centre and had never played full-back in his life but Graham Henry clearly wanted to take a look at him there. It turned out to be a one-off.

There was a great sense of anticipation before the opening match.

A record crowd of over 20,000 turned up at the WACA, the famous cricket ground. Scott Quinnell scored our first try in the opening couple of minutes, which pleased Neil Jenkins no end. We had a sweepstake running on the first try scorer. I had Rob Howley.

The touchdowns came thick and fast for the rest of the game. There were 18 from the Lions in all as Scott went on to score a hat-trick, and so did Dan Luger. We were sitting in the stand, loving it. The home supporters were left to clutch at straws. When Robbie Barugh scored their second try, an Australian guy turned round triumphantly to Johnno, who was near me, and shouted, 'How do you like them apples?' The score was 83–10 at that stage.

Western Australia were mainly enthusiastic amateurs and the gulf between them and full-time professionals showed but they were better than the scoreline suggested – 116–10 was a big win in anybody's book. Plenty of people have scored centuries at the WACA but not many rugby teams.

Ronan O'Gara scored 26 points with his 13 conversions and would have broken Gavin Hastings' Lions record if he had managed to score the try he came close to scoring. That failure spawned a tour bus song, composed by Austin Healey, to the tune of 'Walking in a Winter Wonderland'. It went:

> There's only one Ronan O'Gara.
> If he'd gone a bit farther
> To score a try
> And make Hastings cry
> He'd be living in a record wonderland.

We couldn't have asked for a much better start and after all the intensive work we had done it was a relief just to have a game under our belts. It was difficult to gauge exactly how well we had done – Graham Henry gave the side six out of ten. Complacency was not an option. As soon as the game was over, the players were analysing areas where we might improve for the tougher challenges to come.

There was one major casualty – Simon Taylor. The Scotland No. 8 had been a surprise choice for the tour in many observers' minds but he had shown his athletic talent when he came on as a half-time substitute. Unfortunately, he damaged his knee and our doctor James Robson had to tell him his tour was over before it had hardly begun.

Simon, who is a very quiet lad who kept himself to himself, was able to make his mark off the pitch as well. We went out for a team meal at a pizza restaurant and someone told the staff it was his birthday. A stream of waitresses duly trailed in with a cake and sang happy birthday to him. Needless to say, it wasn't his birthday.

After the Western Australia game he flew with us across Australia to Townsville where he said goodbye. He must have been feeling bad but he put on a brave face.

It is hard to get your head around the size of Australia. I had been before on an England 18-Group trip and England's ill-fated Tour to Hell in 1998, as well as the Centenary Test the following year, but I'd never flown coast to coast. We were in the air for eight hours. That came on top of a six-hour delay at the airport. Dan Luger and I killed some time by investing a few dollars in an ancient arcade video game but the inevitable appearance of the film crew broke my concentration. The management decided to take us off to a casino where a lot of the boys had a flutter. The flight itself passed quite speedily thanks to a marathon card game with Will Greenwood, Dan Luger and Phil Greening. There was no betting involved, just a silly name for the loser. Roger the Cabin Boy and Spurt Reynolds are a couple of the more printable ones. By the time the jokes wore thin we were nearly there and we eventually checked into our hotel at 2 a.m.

Queensland was more like the Australia we had expected – hot. It was also rugby territory. The hard work continued. Martin Corry joined up with the party as a replacement for Simon. He came from England's tour of North America and stepped straight off the plane into lineout practice. Gordon Bulloch joined the squad direct from holiday in Colorado in place of Phil Greening whose knee had gone in training. Phil stayed on in Australia on the off-chance that he might recover and be able to rejoin the party but he never did.

It was a rate of attrition that was to continue for the remainder of the tour. Some people said we must have been over-physical in training but it would have been foolhardy to approach a series against Australia at half throttle. That would have been a very dangerous game to play. It was outright bad luck that we picked up the injuries we did.

Mine, however, was improving and I expected to be on the bench for our first game on the east coast, against a Queensland President's XV. I had to bide my time but there were some distractions while I waited. A couple of days before the game, Jason Robinson, Blackie and I decided to go to see *Pearl Harbor* together at a cinema near the hotel. Unfortunately, when we arrived it was closed. We figured there must be another one within walking distance so we set off towards town. On the way, some English backpackers came up to us and asked us to sign a few things for them. As we were doing so, a woman who was walking past eating a sandwich stumbled badly on a paving stone. She just managed to stay upright and avoid plastering food all over her face. Having asked for directions, we eventually found another cinema 25 minutes' walk away. By the time we arrived, *Pearl Harbor* had already been on for an hour and ten minutes.

Undeterred, Blackie bought tickets and sweets for himself and his 'two sons' and in we went. The cinema was dark inside but it was clearly pretty full. Blackie set off down one aisle with his sweets doing a silly walk. Having found no spaces, he set off down another and suddenly performed a comedy stumble, like the woman with the sandwich, only he went the whole hog. He hit the deck and rolled over three times. Jason and I were in hysterics as he picked up his sweets and calmly took a seat. We went to join him but within minutes he was sound asleep. He woke up for the last 15 minutes, promptly declared it to have been the best film he'd ever seen and left. That was my first night out of the tour.

We were expected to win against the Queensland President's XV although perhaps not quite by the margin we did. They included 12 players with Super-12s experience but we still won 83–6, despite the unnerving presence of a massive spider in the changing room.

There was a terrific atmosphere at the game. The Lions fans were chirpy and those of us not playing were watching from the stand, surrounded by vocal and opinionated Australian supporters. The home side put in some heavy hits early on and when Jason lost the ball in a tackle, one of them piped up with, 'Who is this Robinson? Go back to rugby league.' By halfway through the second half it was difficult not to give them some grief back. Jason had scored five tries. Rob Henderson managed a hat-trick and plenty of others touched down as well. Considering we had led just 10–6 at the interval, it was a fine result.

It was Brisbane next and the Queensland Reds, Super-12s semi-finalists. The business end of the tour was about to begin.

Before we left we had our first senior players' committee meeting at Townsville Airport. Concerns centred around the facilities in the team room and the need to have food on hand immediately after training. The supply had been inconsistent. There were also some worries that the supporters, who were swelling in number all the time, were getting into team rooms and meal rooms. We needed some space at our hotels to relax. There was no mention of training overload although some players did say they were keen to be given more time off for non-rugby activities.

It wasn't as if there was no room for fun. One game, called Red Ass, was a type of tag table tennis with forfeits. Half a dozen players would take it in turns to knock the ball over the net, drop the bat for the next person and race round to the other side. Each time a player messed up he was awarded a letter: R first of all, then E, then D until Red Ass had been spelt out. The first one to get all the letters had to line up against a wall, pull his shorts down and be spanked by everyone else's bat. You see where the name comes from? The big losers were Scott Murray and Malcolm O'Kelly. Austin lost as well but he ran off before his punishment could be dished out.

We were also given the chance to do some unusual sightseeing in a tank full of sharks at Underwater World. I decided to take it. For once kicking practice could wait – I did it in the evening instead. Richard Hill, Neil Back, Martin Corry and I went along and were fitted out in wetsuits. Mine was a particularly feminine affair, which I wasn't too happy with. Iain Balshaw saw the pictures later and called me Scuba Steve, a character from the film *Big Daddy*, for the rest of the tour.

We were weighted down so we could walk along the bottom of the 3 metre deep tank, and after a crash course from the instructors, we lowered ourselves into the underwater chamber. The advice was simple – fold your hands in front of you and keep still. That's not as simple as it sounds with sharks drifting by inches from your face. They were 10ft long nursing sharks, a docile type that breathe through their mouths.

It was scary at first but as I got used to the experience, it became quite therapeutic down there in another world. It was certainly a good way of escaping from rugby. Thinking about moves was the last thing on my mind with those razor-sharp teeth so close. The sharks would swim up to you then at the last second veer off, and the other little fish would nibble your feet.

We were underwater for 20 minutes in all but at one point I had to come back up because my mask fogged up. I made my way to the steps and put my hand down to haul myself up. The step felt strangely spongy for stone and I looked down to find my hand on a shark's back.

The shark looked up at me but seemed pretty relaxed about the whole thing.

Having survived that experience in one piece, I retuned to rugby. A momentous occurrence lay just around the corner. I was about to become a Lion.

chapter thirteen

The Lions roar

Queensland Reds was a tough match for my first game in two months. John Eales was missing, as was Chris Latham and Ben Tune, but they had plenty of other top-quality talent. Nine Wallabies were included. With lots of new calls to worry about and the added pressure of my Lions debut, I was very nervous. I needed reassurance.

Sometimes I just want the match to be over. I am desperate for someone to come up to me and tell me everything turns out all right. No one can. Despite all the hours, weeks and months of preparation, I don't think I'll ever feel totally in control. People often tell me they would love to be doing what I do but if they knew some of the gut-wrenching feelings they might think twice.

My room-mate Rob Howley told me Gareth Edwards had once spoken to the Wales squad before an international. He said: 'I know what you're thinking, "Is it all worth it?" The answer is "yes".' That hit the nail on the head for me. The answer will always be 'yes'. It was helpful to talk to Rob about the anxiety he goes through before a game. I had a similar chat with Mike Catt before a Six Nations game. It can't stop the tension, but it helps prevent you from feeling alone. If two guys like Rob Howley and Mike Catt can feel like that too, it is reassuring.

Queensland was a night match, which gave me extra time to chew over what lay ahead. I tried to sleep during the day to escape from the nerves but when I woke up it was like flicking a switch. They were there again. I watched *Men of Honour*, an excellent film, that afternoon on TV to take my mind off it.

We gathered in the hotel just before 5 p.m. There was a special moment before we left for Ballymore. I was presented with my first Lions shirt. We all had to wait until just before our first match to receive the famous red shirt from Donal in front of the rest of the squad. 'Congratulations,' he said. I felt ten feet tall.

I soon came down to earth. Room for our pre-game preparations was non-existent. When we arrived at Ballymore there was a curtain-raiser taking place so with no room to kick, I went on to the training pitch behind the ground with Dave Alred. To say it was badly policed would be an understatement. As we were kicking to each other, fans were streaming across between us on their way to the ground. Supporters were catching the kicks. It was like the Nike advert with Andre Agassi and Pete Sampras playing tennis in the street. Sometimes there is no rhyme or reason to it all. Despite the pre-match chaos, my goalkicking went well with seven successes out of eight.

The first half as a whole went well. We played some really good rugby in opening up a comfortable lead. I set up Dan Luger for one try with a cross-kick that he did well to take because he said he couldn't see it under the lights. I also managed to put Richard Hill over for another try with a flat inside pass. He runs some great lines and often people don't see him coming. He's our very own invisible man.

We tried out most of our repertoire. There was no plan to hide any moves with Australia in mind. We wanted to test them out, decide what worked well and reuse or modify the successful ones.

The hard part for me was playing with people I wasn't used to. I didn't know how they liked to run on to the ball or what lines they took. I had a couple of problems with Rob Henderson at first. Rob is very vocal and likes to get his own ideas across, which is good because sometimes a centre can see something that a fly-half can't. However, he would want the backs to do one thing and I would have to overrule him. I had the forwards to think of as well and if the call was changed without them knowing, it would have left them out of position. Once we had straightened out the initial difficulties our partnership went very well and it was one I really enjoyed.

With Brian O'Driscoll I found the best approach was just to let him get on with it. It was pointless pre-planning too much because he is the sort of player who is best served using his immense talent spontaneously. Just give him the ball in space and he will do the rest. He is such an exciting bloke to play with.

I half opened up a hole for Brian to score a try four minutes into the second half, and he did the rest, but for the remainder of the game we were largely on the back foot as we lost concentration and Queensland showed us how effectively they could retain possession. Our skill levels let us down when the ball became slippery as the evening dew came down. Our defence held up quite well with only a charged-down kick from Matt Dawson's attempted clearance giving Sam Cordingley a try.

Afterwards Johnno said he wasn't happy with several aspects of our game, particularly the number of turnovers. He felt the referee Stuart Dickinson had allowed a lot of competition for the ball on the floor, which was something we were going to have to become accustomed to if it was to be mirrored in the Tests.

We also took some criticism from Eddie Jones, the coach-in-waiting of the Wallabies. He accused us of being over-physical off the ball, which was nonsense. As the Sky TV man of the match, I was taken off to the press conference after the game and questioned about foul play. We were there to play hard but within the rules. We had to stand up for ourselves if the opposition went below the belt but the idea that we had been told to go out and rough up Queensland was ridiculous. It was never mentioned.

I was happy with how the match had gone for me. I had a lot of new calls and moves to think about, which I found mentally tiring, and a very physical set of opponents in front of me. I took a real clattering setting up Dan's try but I felt I came through the game in good shape.

Then came Australia A at Gosford and a setback. The Lions had gone into the game a touch cold, never having seen the stadium because we were based in Manly, an hour and a half away. I know I would have found that difficult if I had been playing.

The Lions were outplayed although we fought back well late on with tries from Matt Perry and Jason Robinson to narrow the gap to 28–25.

We also lost Mike Catt. His calf and back had been troubling him all tour. He hasn't suffered many injuries because his diet and conditioning are so outstanding, so being sidelined was hard for him. One day he would be able to train, the next he would be struggling again. He felt he had to give it a go in a match situation and it was sad to see him limping away. Catty was missed. As a player, his passing game is integral to the way England play and he would have done an equally good job for the Lions. On a personal level, he looks after me with England, checking everything is OK before and during a game, which I always appreciate.

Near the end, a fan walked past our bench and accused the Lions of not trying. 'I paid $70 for this trip,' he moaned. A few of the lads told him to get lost but Phil Greening took a different tack. 'You got a great deal on your flight, mate,' he said. Most of the support was vibrant but for even one individual to suggest we weren't giving our all was an insult.

Donal spelt out afterwards that if fate decreed we had to lose a match, this was the best one because we still had time to learn from the experience. He stressed there were to be no more defeats.

Some tactical matters had to be sorted out. The half-backs had a big meeting with the hookers to try to improve lines of communication. What had been happening was that the backs would call moves that were impossible to carry out because the forwards weren't supplying the right type of ball. For instance, if from lineouts we wanted to launch our inside-centre at the defence straight from the scrum-half, it meant a huge and looping 35 metre pass if the lineout ball was coming from the No. 2 jumper.

Training remained cursed. Dan Luger swung around in a semi-contact drill, clashed heads with Neil Back and ended up breaking his cheekbone in three places. He was out of the tour. It was desperate luck because Dan was playing superbly, and finishing like the world-class winger he is. It seemed my best mates were cursed, what with Dan, Phil and Catty leaving the party through injury. These guys put so much into preparing to be Lions and for that chance to be taken away through no fault of their own was desperately disappointing. I missed their company.

New recruits were arriving thick and fast. Scott Gibbs, who narrowly missed out on selection in the first place, came in for Mike Catt and Ireland's Tyrone Howe jetted in as a reserve winger.

It was at about this time that the first rumours of discontent started circulating the party, criticising the man-management and the training. One reckoned that 20 players had walked out of a team meeting in protest. I don't know where that came from. Another referred to Colin Charvis who was supposed to have been found on his own in a bar in the Kings Cross area of Sydney, sat down on the floor. He was allegedly drowning his sorrows after being told he would not be featuring in any of the Tests and telling anyone who cared to listen that the management could **** off. He posted a reply on his website saying it was rubbish. He was definitely standing up and he didn't swear!

There were problems and they stemmed from the fact that those who had toured with the Lions in 1997 were coming at it from a different angle. They had been part of a successful tour during which they had trained once a day early in the morning and then been left to their own devices. They wanted more spare time. I love having time off to relax, too, but my mind hardly left rugby for seven weeks.

Any Lions tour is by definition huge but the difference between making history and not doing so is a very small one. Everyone remembers '97 in South Africa but fewer people talk about the '93 tour to New Zealand. Why? On one tour the Lions won the Test series, on the other they lost it. If beating Australia meant giving another half an hour here or there to getting things right, we had to do that. It was understandable that not everybody shared the same viewpoint, as each player's needs are different in order for them to be as fit as possible on matchday but winning a Test series against the world champions has to involve sacrifices. We had to be professional.

We all needed a lift at this point and I got one with the arrival of some familiar faces. I met up with some of my Newcastle colleagues – Stuart Grimes, Andy Mower, Pete Massey and a few others – who had come to Australia via Los Angeles. They had taken great delight in wangling their way into the super-exclusive Beverly Hills Hotel and ordering drinks from the pool in their boxer shorts, and driving a Pontiac Firebird onto the set of a Western. It had been an intense few weeks and it was nice to have a feeling of normality descend, however briefly. My dad and a few of his mates turned up, too. Mum stayed at home, unable to watch the matches even on television until the all-clear had been given from Australia. It was probably just as well she didn't tune in to the second of our Super-12s challenges against Bob Dwyer's New South Wales Waratahs.

We trained for the game at Brookvale Oval where I ran into Brett

Kimmorley and Ben Walker, two of the kickers from the Northern Eagles rugby league team. The last thing Ben said to me was, 'Don't kick your leg off.' They were used to little and often in practice.

As it had happened, I kicked better in the New South Wales match than at any other point on tour, finishing with six out of six. The omens were good before kick-off – I was landing everything. Being close to the crowd, I could sense a pulsating atmosphere building up and the nerves began to worsen. When a punt missed its target by a few yards, one bloke started giving me some serious grief, telling me how badly I was struggling under the pressure.

Our team warm-up session was on the Sydney Cricket Ground, which backed on to the stadium. The contrast was total. In place of the bearpit was an utterly serene backdrop. When we had finished, I stayed behind to put one more kick through the Aussie Rules posts. It was so calm and peaceful. Standing there on my own, half of me wanted to stay where I was. What if I just sat down and didn't go back? I knew I couldn't but that was how I felt. The nerves were so overwhelming and the pressure so enormous that there was a temptation simply to run away from it all. But I took a deep breath, turned round and walked into the most controversial match of the tour.

We won 41–24 but as a game it hit the headlines for all the wrong reasons. It exploded straightaway. Their second row Tom Bowman was yellow-carded for elbowing Danny Grewcock at the kick-off. Later Danny, Phil Vickery, Cameron Blades and Brendan Cannon went in the bin for fighting.

The worst incident surrounded Duncan McRae, the New South Wales full-back. He went berserk, hitting Ronan O'Gara 11 times when he was defenceless on the ground. Ronan needed eight stitches in three separate cuts.

At the press conference, Bob Dwyer suggested the Lions started all the trouble and blamed Danny for sparking it. When it came to our turn, Danny was asked if he felt New South Wales had deliberately come at the Lions. I thought he would play a straight bat but he just said, 'If you mean an elbow in my face after three seconds, then yes, I'd say they did.' I was so surprised I burst out laughing, which was wholly inappropriate in the circumstances.

Thinking about it afterwards, the elbowing incident was weird. It's not a great way to win the ball back but I'm still not sure they had a plan to attack us. I certainly don't think McRae's assault was at all premeditated. The Saracens boys in our squad who knew him well said it was totally out of character.

What happened in that incident was that as Ronan cleared out a ruck perfectly legitimately, he caught McRae in the face with his wrist or forearm. McRae had his head down at the time and obviously thought he had been punched. There was no excuse for his rush of blood but I could see why he might have been a little angry.

When Newcastle played at Bristol earlier in the season, I accidentally whacked their flanker Matt Salter on the nose when I was clearing out a ruck. He started trying to punch me and for my own protection more than anything I threw a few back. After the game I went up to him to apologise – his nose had stopped bleeding by then – but he cut me short by congratulating me on a good shot. I didn't know whether to continue protesting my innocence but I thought I'd play the hard man for once and accepted his praise.

I made a special point of comforting Ronan after the McRae incident. He wasn't a pretty sight and he was feeling quite low. It wasn't the violence that upset him but the fact that he'd had an opportunity taken away by being forced to leave the field. The irony was he had only come on as a replacement for Will Greenwood – the tour's latest casualty with ankle ligament damage.

It was reported afterwards that I had been so shocked by what was going on that I was sick in the changing room at half-time. That's not quite right. I did feel terrible at the interval but it was nothing to do with any punch-ups. All the mental and physical strain of playing flat-out kicked in when I stopped and I wanted to be sick. It happens to me now and again. This time I couldn't sit still and the doctor gave me a tablet to combat the nausea. It was a slow release pill that I was supposed to keep in my mouth but I spat it out early in the second half when I made a tackle.

Overall, I quite enjoyed the game, even though I missed a tackle when I was temporarily moved to centre after Will went off. There was one especially good memory from the night. I managed my first try in a Lions shirt, one of five we scored. It came from a loop around Neil Back and a sprint down the outside. There's no answer to raw pace!

If the rough stuff from New South Wales was meant to distract us ahead of the first Test, it had the opposite effect. It brought us closer together. The fallout continued in the media for quite a while but we had no time to reflect. We were on our way to Coffs Harbour to prepare for the big game.

Ironically in such a huge country, we were staying a couple of miles from the Wallabies but we never came across them. We said goodbye to Lawrence here. His knee had never come right and it flared up again against New South Wales, which meant an operation back home. There isn't much you can say in this situation. A bloke has dedicated himself for months, maybe years, for the chance to play in a Lions Test and suddenly it is taken away by pure bad luck. I tried to imagine how I would have felt but I couldn't. It would have been too much to bear.

David Wallace was the latest call-up, which was especially good news for him as he was on his way to an Ireland training camp in Poland. Dorian West had already detoured from his holiday to replace Robin McBryde.

Before the tour, we had all spoken of the next match being the most important and the need to avoid a divide between the Test and non-Test teams. In Coffs Harbour that broke down.

There was only a week remaining to get things right for the first Test and if the side wanted to taper down training as kick-off approached, as much as possible had to be crammed in early on in the week. With attention being focused on the Test, the players picked for the midweek game against New South Wales Country were marginalised. Two days before the match, instead of fine-tuning their preparations, they were asked to pretend to be the Wallabies in training so the Test team could practise against their moves. They were not hugely impressed. I wouldn't have been in their position. They felt they were being robbed of a chance to prove what they could do in terms of Test selection. The amount of training was still a problem, too.

The whole business came up in a brief senior players' committee meeting in Donal's room. The management's response was that they were fully aware of the concerns but that the intensity had to be kept high to ready ourselves for the Wallabies.

Being picked for the midweek game against New South Wales Country at Coffs Harbour was unlikely to bring good news regarding Test selection. With the sell-out at the Gabba only four days away, players in the midweek side were set to miss out. The surprise name in the side was Iain Balshaw. Most people would have picked him as the favourite for the No. 15 shirt when we set off for Australia. With that call, Matt Perry moved into pole position, and never surrendered the jersey.

Balsh wasn't at his very best during the tour. He didn't play badly at all but the openings he found so regularly for England weren't there for him in Australia. He blamed the Lions style and I think he missed Mike Catt. As well as creating room for himself, he is also at his best when someone gives him half a yard of space to work in and Catty's exceptional game reading and passing does that with Bath and England.

Any discontent was nipped in the bud by a genuine tragedy. Neil Back and I had just returned to our hotel from a long walk along the beach front. We had been chatting about the tour and how it was panning out. He is a great bloke to talk to because he is so positive. He never even mentioned the rib injury he was secretly carrying from the New South Wales game. As we wandered back to the hotel having put the world to rights, we saw a lot of people rushing the other way. We asked what was happening and were told one of our party was in trouble.

We sprinted back down to the beach where an ambulance was parked and a crowd of people were surrounding someone. It was Anton Toia, one of the liaison men supplied by the Australian Rugby Union. He was dead. He had been out whale watching with some of the squad. The boat had dropped them off about 30 feet out to sea and they had swum back to the beach but Anton had a heart attack and never made it.

A Kiwi, he was a very popular member of the back-up team. He had helped with all the unheralded jobs such as making the drinks and generally worked his socks off for the Lions. He had driven me to kicking practice and now here he was lying on the beach. It was the first dead body I'd ever seen.

We were all shocked that something so tragic could have happened. That night's team meeting was cancelled and the players stood for a minute's silence and wore black armbands in his honour at the midweek game. We had a collection for his funeral.

We won comfortably enough against New South Wales Country, 46–3, but it wasn't our best performance.

Next morning the Test side was announced. It was a tense moment as Donal ran through the names. I never presumed I would be in – I've seen too many people bitten for that – so to hear 'Wilkinson' was great. However much the experience of being a Lion may mean, the Test matches are the ones everyone desperately wants to play in. As soon as I knew I was in, my thoughts turned to the game. The pressure was on immediately.

As the Coffs Harbour selection had suggested, Matt Perry was in at full-back ahead of Balsh with Rob Howley partnering me at half-back. There was no Neil Back because of his ribs, which meant a place for his Welford Road chum Martin Corry. Jason Robinson's dazzling try-scoring feats – eight in four games – had helped catapult him to the front of the queue. It meant he would start a game for the Lions before he had started one for England. The full side read: Perry; James, O'Driscoll, Henderson, Robinson; Wilkinson, Howley; Smith, Wood, Vickery, Johnson, Grewcock, Corry, Hill, Quinnell.

The hype surrounding the match was incredible. I tried to avoid it by steering clear of newspapers and television news but it was difficult to miss. The series was creating ripples around the sporting world. Pat Rafter wore a gold headband at Wimbledon, while Tim Henman brought a Lions shirt along to one of his press conferences. Tickets were like gold dust. We were all allocated two free ones and were given an option of buying four more. I took all six and promised them to Dad and his mates. I was lying in bed in the early hours of Thursday morning having just watched a film, when I realised to my horror that I'd left them on a table in the team room.

I was sharing with Rob Howley and we were on Floor 14; the team room was on Floor 30. I shot out of bed and tried to get the lift there but it wouldn't budge. There was no option but to use the stairs. I sprinted up them but when I reached Floor 30 the doors were locked. Panicking, I went back down to 29 and tried to use the lift again. It wouldn't have any of it.

I went down to reception and explained my predicament. They took me through the kitchens to a special lift that would go to Floor 30 and when I went into the team room the tickets were still there. Relieved, I went back to bed. At 2 a.m. I was out of bed again. For some reason my nose had blocked up and I couldn't sleep. I went to find the doctor but couldn't and was forced to endure a very poor night's sleep and lots of stick from Rob.

He was a difficult room-mate in one respect. He is totally the opposite to me in his attitude to all the pre-match build-up. He watches everything related to the game. He likes to pin diagrams of moves and notes on strategies on the bedroom wall. I draw them as well but I keep them in my pocket and peek at them at odd times and in the changing room before the game. We led a strange existence what with Rob devouring every scrap about the game and me walking around with my fingers in my ears and my eyes closed.

We did share the same scepticism about an advert for a massage that was slipped under our door at the Brisbane Sheraton. I think what gave away its authenticity was that it was written on a napkin.

The Lions trained for the first Test at Brisbane Grammar School, which had the most incredible facilities. We also had an unusual walk-through in a small park near our hotel. There were flowerbeds littered about so moves had to be altered to avoid trampling all over them. The water pipes became Wallaby defenders. Petunias aside, training went well although the wind made kicking tricky.

Johnno held his captain's meeting on the Friday at which Alun Carter put together a five-minute sequence of inspirational stuff from the tour so far. The ante was being upped. Phil Greening and Mike Catt, who must both have desperately wished they were there, sent me text messages wishing me the best of luck, which was a nice touch.

On the eve of the first Test, Blackie slipped a note under our doors. It read:

It is said that character is the sum total of what you believe and how you act. The Lions squad have a belief which seems to get stronger daily, and behave in a way that represents all the best changes that have occurred in the game since professionalism took hold six years ago.

You win with good people, good characters who have great determination, enthusiasm, love for the game and, of course, an above average ability to function on the field of play.

If we are to compete successfully on Saturday and emerge as the best, we have to push ourselves and each other harder than ever before. We know the height of this challenge but it's not enough to stare up the steps that will get us there. We must get up those stairs. You personally must be prepared to lead the way and take that first step.

We are prepared, we have our plan. During the course of the game we must expect the unexpected and react positively and with great assurance to anything they throw at us.

On Saturday, when you've worked so hard that you feel you may pass out and your body and mind seem to have been stretched to breaking point, and momentarily you think you've no more left to give, hear a voice remind you that there's something far more important than anyone's susceptibility to pain. It is the great tradition, belief and respect of what it takes to be a true Lion. It is then you will become a legendary Lion.

Three hours before the game, the shirts were handed out at our hotel by Willie John McBride, a Lions legend. Each of us went up individually, shook hands and received our shirt from him. He spoke of past Lions and his experiences in the shirt, of the intense challenge and how good the Australians were and the immense honour of playing for our four countries. Most of all, he underlined the great feeling winning would bring. It was stirring oratory and really got the butterflies going.

As we came down the escalator to leave the hotel, there were hundreds of fans waiting for us, chanting 'Lions, Lions'. We were used to it at games but in a hotel lobby, it took us aback. The support was fantastic.

The bus was quiet on the way to the Gabba – no music, little conversation, just our own private thoughts of what lay ahead. When we arrived I went out to kick and was immediately hit by a sea of red. It felt like a home game. The Lions supporters – 15,000 in a crowd of 37,000 – made a terrific noise.

We had initially been refused permission to practise on the pitch but we pushed and they eventually allowed it. This hadn't been communicated to one official who came up and told us no kicking was allowed.

'Yeah, whatever,' I said and just carried on. You can't let this sort of thing affect your concentration.

'There's only one Jonny Wilkinson,' the Lions fans sang as I went through my routine and then 'Jonny, Jonny, give us a wave.' I didn't. I always think it looks a bit wrong when you are supposed to be concentrating on something else.

The team warm-up was indoors in a compact space, which worked well. It was noisy and close-knit. There was a last word from Graham Henry, then it was just the 15 of us. We broke off from our huddle and I took one last look at our moves. I spoke to Rob Howley and Rob Henderson, the two players either side of me on the pitch, to double-check everything and then Johnno led us out. What a roar!

In the heat of the moment, I needed a cool head. I had been striking the ball a bit tinnily in warm-up so I decided to hit one more well for the sake of my confidence. However, when we arrived on the pitch I found lots of young girls stretching flags out on the ground just where I wanted to kick from. I lined the ball up anyway and the ones in the firing line laughed nervously. Here I was, seconds before the most important game of my life, and I was having this vision of scuffing the ball badly, connecting with one of the girls and being booed by the crowd. It was quite surreal.

Fortunately, I hit it OK and it went through the posts just as the Wallabies ran out. Their line-up was predictably strong. They had gone for Nathan Grey's power at inside-centre and the extra bulk of Owen Finegan at blind-side flanker. Otherwise the side picked itself.

We lined up for the anthems, sorry anthem – the Lions don't have one, which seems a little unfair – and then we were away.

The series could not have started much better. There were three minutes on the clock when Rob Howley, myself and Matt Perry worked the ball out to Jason Robinson on the left wing who left Australia's full-back Chris Latham clutching at thin air as he went over for our opening try. We had been encouraged to play it as we saw it once we had established our structure and with a four on three advantage we used it. Give Jason a situation like that and he is almost unstoppable. Matt Perry says if you are the last line of defence in training, you just have to guess which way he will go because his step is so devastating. If you choose wrongly, you miss him by about five metres!

It got better. We knew Finegan was not the quickest off the mark and we felt we could exploit that at the scrum. We practised bringing Brian O'Driscoll and Jason – two of our best strike runners – around his side and trying to outstrip him. The move was called Pace and we pulled it off to perfection. It worked a treat with a try, the two of them putting Dafydd James in with five minutes of the half remaining.

We had a wonderful start to the second half, too. Brian O'Driscoll surged in between Nathan Grey and Jeremy Paul, left Matt Burke behind and went in from 50 metres. There was less than a minute on the clock. When Scott Quinnell went over for our fourth try, the score was an unbelievable 29–3.

This was the side with the best defence in the world. We had worked hard on moving the ball through several phases so that we could line up mismatches – wings against props, that sort of thing – but this was as good as we could have hoped for.

Only then did Australia post a warning of what they would throw at us in the rest of the series. They kept the ball for much of the remainder of the game and worked tries for Andrew Walker and

Nathan Grey when we were down to 14 men after Phil Vickery was sin-binned and then Martin Corry.

Still, 29–13 was quite a scoreline at the end and if four out of seven wasn't quite what I was looking for from my kicking (the three I missed were very difficult), I was delighted with how the game had gone overall. Rob Howley was a joy to play alongside. He has a lot of pace and is not afraid to have a go. When he chooses to pass, he sometimes takes the ball around the corner of the ruck that pulls in the defence and tends to give his fly-half and back line extra numbers.

The only downside from the game was that Colin Charvis, who had come on as a substitute, was banned for two games after being cited by the match commissioner Steve Hinds for use of the knee in clearing out a ruck.

The boys were chuffed but we knew we could not treat it as anything more than the first step in a three-match series. I went out late for a walk to a bar called City Rowers on the front where I met some friends. Some space had been set aside for the Lions. It was mad in there. We were given our own bar separated by a flimsy row of plants and every so often a fan would fall through the hedge and be politely thrown back by a bouncer. I wangled a passage in for my dad and met up with Pete Massey and Gareth Maclure but after a few lemonades I left them to it and wandered off back to the hotel. The taxi queue was too long so I ended up strolling back on my own, using the name of the hotel on the roof to guide me. It was a strange end to a wonderful night.

chapter fourteen

The pen and the sword

After the first Test, the Australian press ripped into their team for their performance. We had our own problems to deal with. On the morning of the first Test, the *Daily Telegraph* printed a column written earlier by Matt Dawson expressing his dissatisfaction at various aspects of the tour. They ranged from claims about the dubious inspirational qualities of Graham Henry to the huge amount of training we were doing. He said Donal Lenihan was treating us like children and criticised Andy Robinson and Phil Larder for being too distant. Matt even wrote that some players were thinking of leaving the tour.

I had got wind of it the day before, but the importance of the occasion swept it to one side until afterwards. On the morning after the match, Matt stood up at a team meeting in the hotel and explained himself. He said he had let himself down and felt he might have affected morale. He added that he was entitled to his own views but that he had no right to air them publicly. If people wanted to call him this and that, they could. Jokingly, a few immediately did so. Donal said that Matt would probably be fined and he was.

I know Matt well and was sympathetic. He had come across as a very different person from the team man he is. As for his criticisms, the attack on Graham Henry was probably the most serious. Each to their own, I suppose, but I did find him inspirational.

Graham was a controversial choice in the first place as a New Zealander but his accent made no difference to his coaching. He wasn't a robot either – he became quite emotional at times because he so badly wanted to win.

What differed from the approach I was used to was his final team-talk before matches. He was quite detailed in the way he spelt out what he wanted. I was on edge by that point anyway so I didn't need huge encouragement but I, like some of the others, preferred something more general to stir us up for the battle ahead.

Graham was mature enough not to bear grudges. He picked Matt at scrum-half for the third Test and gave him the kicking duties for the next game against the ACT Brumbies in Canberra. Matt produced the perfect thank-you by landing the last kick of the match to steal victory.

It was a fantastic comeback by the boys after underperforming and trailing early on against a side lacking a lot of its Super-12 stars. It was crowned by Austin Healey's try after the final hooter. Play continues after the hooter sounds until the ball is dead – something I am not sure whether I like yet – but the boys kept playing and playing until they worked an opening for Austin. He managed to slide in a bit closer to the posts but it was still a massive pressure kick for Matt and he held his nerve superbly. We all rushed down to the changing room to congratulate Matt but he was so drained after a terrible week and all the tension he could hardly lift his head up. He just slumped there in his cubicle.

The game was the occasion of a further souring of relations between Austin and their towering second row Justin Harrison. The two had almost come to blows when the Lions played Australia A, and they were at it again at Bruce Stadium. It all stemmed from a misunderstanding. Austin intercepted a pass on halfway and with a clear run in, checked with the referee to see if he was onside. Harrison thought his gesture was intended to say 'look at me' and barged into him after he had touched down. ACT were in the lead and Harrison said to Austin, 'That's only one try, you ★★★★★★.' When Austin scored the dramatic second, he replied, 'I guess that makes it two tries and you lose.' Harrison threw his scrum cap at him, which was quite a mild response in the circumstances.

The Test team had flown up to Canberra to support the side. It took a day out of our preparations for the second Test but was important from a squad point of view. I was rooming with Matt Perry. Like me, he usually sleeps for Britain and Ireland but we were both woken up in the early hours by a woman banging on our door, shouting, 'Get up, get up. You're so boring.' Matt crept over to the door in the dark and peered through the spy-hole. I tiptoed over for a look too and saw this 40-year-old leaning over the balcony, shouting at the top of her voice. We don't know who she was but security hauled her off shortly afterwards.

I met some of the Canberra Raiders rugby league team while I was doing kicking practice there. One of them came out with some pretty disparaging stuff about the Australian rugby union players. His viewpoint surprised me as in England I believe there is a mutual respect between the two codes' players, if not always their supporters.

The league players I had met earlier in the trip had been fine. Trent Lee, the North Queensland Cowboys kicker, had been particularly approachable. Here, there seemed to be outright hostility. The rise of rugby union and the forthcoming defections of two outstanding Kangaroos, Wendell Sailor and Mat Rogers, had obviously stirred up some antagonism. We left them to it and headed south for Melbourne, back into Aussie Rules country although you would never have known it. The second Test was everywhere. The 52,000 tickets for the game had sold out in 18 minutes.

I was back rooming with Rob Howley and I had a new policy to combat his rugby junkiness – hiding under the duvet whenever the match was mentioned. If I'd followed this plan to the letter, I would have been in bed 24 hours a day.

To counteract our Red Army, the Australian RFU had issued a plea for their supporters to wear Wallaby colours at the game. They even handed out scarves. At one point I looked out of our massage room and saw a car driving past with a billboard on the side imploring fans to wear gold. It was all miles over the top.

I briefly escaped the madness to visit the Australian Open tennis courts and had a knock-up on number one court with our overworked masseur Richard Wegrzyk. Unfortunately, it wasn't as relaxing as I'd hoped because it turned into another media event.

A lot of the others went off to visit the 'Neighbours' set. Austin got chatting with a couple of the actresses and asked if they were coming to the game. 'If you can get us tickets,' they said. 'Mmm, whatever,' said Austin as he walked away. The girls were less than impressed with this show of indifference and waved away the team bus when it was time to go with a variety of hand signals that wouldn't have made the final edit. That was another couple of fans in the bag for the weekend.

The second Test was to be played at the Colonial Stadium under a closed roof. We obviously wanted a taste of it beforehand so when we arrived the day before the match to find it shut, we were delighted. We asked the officials to leave it that way so our players could get used to it. They said no. Five minutes after we left, the Australian team turned up and they closed the roof for them. We were not happy.

On the morning of the game they would not let us kick on the pitch, either, so we had to make do with the uncovered training pitch. It had rained heavily and it was boggy underfoot. Conditions could not have been more different from the stadium.

On game night itself, we were finally allowed on to kick but there were huge speakers on the pitch for the pre-match entertainment. I moved one of the wires so I could have a clear run at the ball but as I prepared to kick, an official deliberately dragged it back again. It seemed the Australians would not stop short of anything to square the series. The big screen was showing a taped interview with a raucous Wallaby fan who was screaming how the Lions were going to be beaten and how they would not know what had hit them. They loved his attitude so much they tracked the bloke down inside the stadium and interviewed him again.

Finally, as we were about to kick-off after the singing of 'Advance Australia Fair', we were forced to wait while they sang 'Waltzing Matilda'. It would be fair to say they stacked the odds as heavily as they could, and it paid off.

I thought we played really well in the first half but we just couldn't open up a big enough lead, despite the number of breaks and opportunities we created. An 11–6 advantage, including a Leicester-style lineout try from Neil Back who was fit again, was not enough. Still, more of the same in the second half and the series would have been ours. It was there for the taking.

Unfortunately, it all fell apart and Australia swamped us, at least on the scoreboard, 35–14. The catalyst was an interception try from Joe Roff after 30 seconds. It was my pass he picked up. Even when Roff intervened we almost had enough space in which to haul him back but he managed to get to the try-line. Given my time again, I would still have thrown that pass. You have to play it how you see it on the pitch and I felt it was on.

We gave away another soft try later when the Australians took one of our scrums and John Eales picked up the loose ball. The wheel we had on for our intended attack opened up the field for them.

The game was effectively over when I made a tackle on Daniel Herbert with 10 minutes left and immediately feared the worst. As my leg swung round it was accidentally caught by Owen Finegan and I thought it had broken. I couldn't feel my toes and as I lay there I was afraid of what I might see if I looked down. The stretcher was called for and arrived on a cart. I didn't want to try to stand up. All I could think of was the footballer Gary Mabbutt trying to take a couple of steps on an injured leg and the bone snapping under his weight. As the cart took me off down the tunnel, the Australian fans hurled abuse at me. Give me a break, I thought. By then I was just beginning to feel a couple of toes again.

I was taken to hospital for an X-ray. It showed no break, just severe bruising. My thoughts immediately turned to the decisive third Test in a week's time. Would I be fit? The doctors were cautiously optimistic, if I could stop the bleeding in the muscle causing problems.

I was joined in casualty by Rob Howley, whose tour was ended by confirmation of a broken rib, and Richard Hill who had been caught in the face by Nathan Grey and concussed. The X-ray showed Hilly's skull is a centimetre thicker than average, which was a source of great hilarity to the rest of the team.

I may have endured the odd difficulty with Australian fans but their medics were wonderful. They immersed my foot in a plaster cast and told me to keep it up at 45 degrees for the next two days. Do nothing, they instructed, and I ran up a £250 room bill watching endless films and filling my face with room service. The ARU kindly paid.

The advice worked wonders. By the time I flew off to join up with the rest of the squad in Sydney with the cast removed, I was pretty sure I would be fit. I tried not to sound too over-confident when I spoke to the press as I arrived at the Manly Pacific Hotel, but I was already preparing myself for the epic decider at the Olympic Stadium on Saturday night.

I fought my way back to fitness with three physio sessions and three pool sessions each day. They started at 8.30 a.m. in the hotel pool on the roof. It seemed to rain most of the time and the water temperature was pretty cold so it wasn't exactly pleasurable but the icy waters did the trick.

After sitting out the early sessions along with Rob Henderson, Brian O'Driscoll, Neil Back, Austin Healey and Scott Quinnell, I took my place again in training on Thursday. We were a battered and bruised party but the size of the challenge was driving us on for one last effort.

Yet another setback was in store on this injury-jinxed trip when Austin, who had been brought in for Dafydd James, dropped out with serious back muscle spasms the day before the game. His replacement on the wing was straightforward enough – Dafydd slotted in – but with Rob Howley out of the tour, it left us without scrum-half cover on the bench. Scotland captain Andy Nicol was dragged away from leading a fans' tour party to do the job. He had 24 hours to learn all the calls and reacquaint himself with the feel of a rugby ball. It wasn't ideal but Rob and I gave him all the calls and hoped Matt Dawson made it through the game.

Austin's withdrawal had a desperate knock-on effect for Mark Taylor. Because we needed a specialist scrum-half on the bench, it meant someone had to draw the short straw and lose their place. Mark was the one who had to go. His chance of a Test appearance had disappeared thanks to a cruel twist of fate he did not deserve. I told him how sorry I was and he just shrugged and said it wasn't meant to be. That was Mark all over. He was great to be with all tour, joking all the time and he played well whenever he was given an opportunity.

The Wallabies also had injury problems after an immensely physical second Test. Stephen Larkham was missing. He was a hugely influential player for Australia and we had been accused of targeting him in the first two Tests. Let's just say we didn't miss any opportunities to put him down hard when we were within range. As the playmaker, this sort of attention goes with the territory. I know if people get hold of me, they're not likely to go easy. Elton Flatley was his replacement, and Austin's old mate Justin Harrison was in for his debut in place of the injured David Giffin.

I was surprised to see Andrew Walker included in the line-up. When I was in hospital, he was there as well for an X-ray on a jaw injury. He couldn't speak too well. Somehow his X-ray got put in with the Lions' ones and our doctor James Robson thought he saw a break.

Australian coach Rod Macqueen played a masterstroke. He brought forward his retirement to make this his final game in charge. If the Wallabies did not do it for themselves, or their country, they could always do it for their coach.

The initiative had switched to Australia. However, we were confident we could do it. We had won the first Test handsomely, played well in the first half the previous week and only lost the match by giving up a couple of bad tries after the interval. The management stressed that we had to be more clinical and aggressive. The idea was to use our kicking game and play our rugby in their half of the field. A lot of our second Test errors had come in our own half and with the ball so contestable that had led to turnovers.

It was interesting to see how rugby had developed in the space of a season. Sides had gone from leaving attackers to keep the ball for phase after phase, to trying everything they could to get their hands on it. Australia would often wait until they had been warned twice by the referee before letting go after a tackle.

The tactical side was one thing, the emotional quite another. The whole tour had come down to one match – 80 minutes. Would we go down in history as winners or losers? There were 15,000 Lions supporters in Australia banking on our performances and millions more back home. All we could do was play for each other. The bond that had been formed back in Hampshire almost two months ago was still intact despite all the trials and tribulations of the tour. It was time for another pre-match note from Blackie.

Thanks for your contributions on this tour. Some have been outstanding, some possibly a bit wide of the mark, myself very much included. But all our efforts were, and are, well-intentioned towards the 2001 Lions cause. If we know this in our hearts, we can be justifiably proud. Thanks to us all from us all.

And so to the final countdown. As Johnno said, 'In 24 hours' time, turn up in the most determined mindset you've ever experienced.' If you answer Johnno's personal plea, we will win because as Andy Robinson said, 'You are the most talented and best players I've ever worked with.'

Graham echoed, 'You will win because you are the best team.'

Three of the leaders in this Lions party are screaming it, boys – absolute belief in our abilities.

Johnno's determination is so strong and vivid. A great gridiron coach summed up the effect of determination like this: 'Most players are about as effective as they make their minds up to be.' How right he was. Make your mind up.

There was also a selection of quotes and poems including 'If' by Rudyard Kipling, and a thought from Albert Einstein: 'Your imagination is a preview of life's coming attractions.'

This sort of material, for me, was inspirational. I was ready.

On the night, Donal handed the shirts out at the ground and spoke for about quarter of an hour. It was passionate stuff but I was nervous and I couldn't concentrate. I was impatient to get out into the stadium and kick. My leg wouldn't keep still.

When I returned we went through the familiar routine. It ended, as it always does, with Johnno. Before he leads the side out into the tunnel, he always stops, turns round and gives us a final motivating word. This time he reminded us that we were about to embark on a once in a lifetime experience. There was no turning back.

I wonder what soldiers feel when they go to war. It must be a massively enhanced version of the adrenaline and fear we experience before a match like this. Of course for them it is a matter of life and death rather than winning or losing. I know it is only a rugby match but in those few moments it is all-embracing – invigorating and frightening at the same time.

Out we went. The support had become more vociferously pro-Australian with each Test; in the Olympic Stadium we really were in the Wallabies' backyard. The Lions fans were out in greater force than ever but thrown together in the worst seats in a crowd of 84,188 they were dwarfed by the Australian contingent. It was us against the world champions and us against the world. We had to endure another dose of 'Waltzing Matilda', which a couple of Lions fans tried to sabotage by throwing a towel over the microphone – they obviously felt the same about it as we did – and then we were away.

In the other Tests we started well and scored first. This time the Wallabies were out of the blocks quicker than us with a couple of penalties. I wasn't worried. We struck back with a converted try – inevitably from Jason Robinson – after some great handling from Tom Smith and Keith Wood. I had spotted that we had numbers out left and switched the play. It worked well.

Australia regained the initiative with the first of Daniel Herbert's two tries and it looked as if they would go in at half-time with a handy lead, but after a couple of misses I managed to put over an important penalty to cut the deficit. We were three points down at the break.

We were supposed to change our shirts at half-time – it was meant to symbolise a fresh start – but I was so caught up in the game I forgot.

Even though we lost Scott Quinnell at the interval, the second half began well. We were camped on their line and pressing hard for a try. As the ball came out from Matt, I was aware I had a couple of players on my inside and hesitated to see if a pass back was on. It wasn't, so I feigned to cut back inside myself, stood up to Toutai Kefu and saw a hole to the line open up for me. I scored. The try was testament to the work I had done on my agility with Steve Black and my brother. Dodging around a heavy swinging punchbag in the gym had brought its rewards.

It was nip and tuck throughout the second half but Australia managed to withstand the 10 minute loss of Herbert for a high tackle on Brian O'Driscoll, and edged ahead with quarter of an hour left. With 10 minutes remaining it was 29–23. I never felt desperate. I always thought we would do it but we were still unable to string enough phases together to run at a disorganised defence.

With two minutes left a chink of light appeared – we were awarded a penalty on halfway. Johnno told me to kick it as close to the corner flag as I could. Woody had already called the lineout before I struck it. It was the right decision. Our lineout drives had gone well all evening and from 10 metres out, if the Wallabies decided to pull it down they risked conceding a penalty try. That would have left a conversion to win the match from in front of the posts. Mentally I was already rehearsing the kick I was going to have to win the series. I needed to be ready for the moment when it came.

It never did. Justin Harrison produced the leap of his life and pinched the ball off Johnno at the front. The crowd went mad but even then I was still upbeat. They had cleared to touch and we still had good field position. As the buzzer sounded we still had possession down the right and for once the Australian defence was disorganised. Balsh and Colin Charvis, on as substitutes, kept the ball in. If we could only work it back across field we were in with a shout. But one of their guys got a hand to it and they put the ball into touch – game over, series lost, desolation.

We had put so much of ourselves into those seven and a half weeks, so much effort, enthusiasm and pride, and all for nothing. It didn't matter that I'd scored a try, it was irrelevant that we'd won the first Test. We had lost the series, end of story.

I returned to the dressing room and my unused Lions shirt was still hanging there. Later, the players all signed it for me but at that time no one said a word. There was nothing to say. Blackie put his arm round me and offered his consolation as we went back out on to the pitch for the presentations. 'I still love you,' he said.

I covered my eyes, not because I was crying but to keep the cameras from prying. It was a very personal moment and I needed my privacy. Rod Macqueen told the crowd it was 'bloody great' to be an Australian; at that moment, it was bloody awful to be a losing Lion.

So why did we lose? I missed a couple of kicks, which was disappointing, but so did Matt Burke. I don't think they were critical. What decided it in my view was how much ball they stole from us in the second half and how many penalties we conceded.

My success rate from kicks was higher in the provincial games than in the Test matches – 71 per cent compared to 57 per cent. People instinctively drew the conclusion that because there is more pressure in the big games, I was affected by it. I disagree. Feeling extra tension is not a reason for missing.

Statistics do not always tell the whole truth and if you compare the kicks I took on in provincial and Test matches it reveals a different picture. Because we were winning the warm-up games, we tended to go for tries rather than penalties, so most of my shots were conversions. In the Tests penalties were always going to play more of a part. My range with the Summit ball was around the 40 metre mark and we would often go for goal from there, safe in the knowledge that if I missed Australia would have to drop out and give us the ball back. In snooker it would be called a shot to nothing.

Throughout the series I thought I struck the ball quite well. If you analyse the first Test, I was fractionally wide with a touchline conversion, just off with a long-range penalty and then hit the flag on top of the post with my third kick. I hadn't really done anything wrong yet found myself nought from three. I landed my next four, including a touchline conversion of Dafydd James's try to finish with four from seven. A statistician might look at a return of less than 60 per cent and dismiss it as below par for me, but I wasn't unhappy. I set myself high standards and I know I could have done little more. Likewise in the third Test. I finished with five out of nine and was pleased with eight of those strikes. Some days they go over, others they don't.

There was a physical element to our defeat. The Wallabies came to the series fresh whereas the Lions were at the end of an exhausting 11-month season in Europe. However, the most important factor was in our heads. Australia won because they had the mental edge. They were a unit used to winning big matches – the bulk of that side had won the World Cup and the Tri Nations. We were still constructing that winning habit. When the chips were down in the third Test, they knew how to close out the match because they had done it as a team so many times before. Australia are used to winning close games. There was nothing else to choose between the two sides over three matches.

Afterwards we headed into Sydney to drown our sorrows. It was light by the time we arrived back. It was then that I finally found Brian O'Driscoll's weakness – play him at table tennis at 8 a.m. after no sleep and a lot of alcohol and he struggles badly to put his game together.

Matt Dawson shared a taxi back with a friend of his and a random Lions fan. The supporter started giving his views on the match. Not being able to see Matt behind him, he was particularly critical of the half-backs. I couldn't kick my goals under pressure apparently and Matt was nowhere near as good as Rob Howley. In fact, he was useless. He was criticised for everything – kicking, running, you name it. When the taxi arrived in Manly, the bloke got out. As he did so, Matt wound the window down and said politely, 'Make sure you have a very good evening.' The bloke's jaw dropped to the pavement. He turned round and ran off into the night.

The plan was to meet up again at 12.30 the next day in the U-Turn bar for an all-day binge. Neil Back and I surfaced at 11.30 and pottered along. It was clear the pace was being forced so, as lightweights, we sneaked off to the beach for the afternoon. We drank hot chocolate together, chatted to supporters and generally chilled out. Then came an urgent text message from Richard Hill. We had to be back in the bar by 7 p.m. Apparently he was struggling badly and needed some even worse drinkers as support. I suggested we hide but Backy reckoned that policy might backfire in the long run so we returned. Hendo, Phil Greening and Woody were leading the singing, Ronan was yelling, 'Ya can't take it,' at anyone who would listen and the party was in full swing. As the 2001 Lions were dissolved, some of the party did dissolve. Ronan was terrific all tour. He has such a professional attitude and he was selfless in his approach – he always had time for others. Like with Jenks, we became firm friends as well as kicking partners. Touring often creates new friendships. I went away hardly knowing Rob Howley or Brian O'Driscoll and returned the best of mates. However, I probably spent more time with Richard Hill, an old friend from England squad sessions, than any other Lion. You think you know people well but the length of the tour revealed more about the characters of good blokes like Richard and Johnno.

There was room for one more piece of controversy. Austin Healey had written a column in the *Guardian* on the morning of the third Test, and the ramifications were about to be felt. The article called Justin Harrison an ape and a plank. I'm sure once Harrison was on the pitch it went out of his mind completely but in the build-up a jibe like that can add an extra dimension to a team's preparations. Austin is a hilarious bloke. He loves a laugh but takes his rugby seriously. If it was Austin who penned this and not his ghostwriter, this was a joke that probably backfired. Rugby should never really become personal. For something like that to be written was tempting fate. It may have made people pick up the paper but your first responsibility as a player is to your team, not your newspaper or your readers. I've been doing columns since I was 19 and I always try to put the team first. Insulting opponents takes some of your strength away and hands it to the other man. A column is a good place to put your personality across and discuss interesting issues but I don't see it as a forum for breaking big stories or creating the news agenda.

Looking back, touring with the Lions was an experience of a lifetime. It was totally different from playing for England because of the Lions' short shelflife. The history, the shirt and the whole business of bringing together players from different countries for a rugby mission made it special. But for me, a great experience isn't enough. Winning is everything and we lost.

It is human nature to wonder how we might have done if all the squad had stayed fit. We lost some wonderful players during the course of the trip and I know from first-hand experience just what Lawrence Dallaglio, Mike Catt and Dan Luger can add to a team. What if . . . ? In years to come the anguish of defeat may wear off and I might remember Australia 2001 as a brilliant tour with great players and good people, but not yet.

What I aim to do is store up the pain and rechannel it into my next big challenge whether that is a Six Nations Championship, a World Cup or the 2005 Lions tour. It will act as my motivation. I'm convinced if I keep being selected, I will end up a winner on the highest stage. Then I'll be able to look back on this Lions tour and say it helped me succeed. Just like England's unbeaten season and Newcastle's Twickenham triumph, it all goes into the pot.

When the moment eventually comes, all the hard work, sacrifice and ultimate disappointment of Sydney will have been worth it.

chapter fifteen

The Lionhearts – my six outstanding tourists

Martin Johnson

Watching Johnno in training before the third Test, Brian O'Driscoll turned to me and remarked, 'He's a hell of an athlete, isn't he?' I'd never really looked at him in that light before. He was always this big leader who was in the team and when he was there you knew you had a much better chance of winning. But he is a tremendous athlete. He also probably trains harder and understands rugby more clearly than anyone else.

I knew he was outstanding before the tour but my respect for him has risen to another level now. As a captain, he didn't waste words but he always spared the time to check up on me despite having so much else on his plate. He was a hugely reassuring presence.

The Lions captain has to be the team's best player and Johnno was right up there every match, leading by example as he always does. If he'd got his way he would have played all the time, but the management wisely held him back before unleashing him. He was outstanding. Our lineout problems meant we were forced to throw to Johnno at the front more often than we wanted but he did the job for us manfully until Justin Harrison's fateful intervention in Sydney.

His weakness is cricket. Sent out to bat in the Manly Pacific Test during the final week, he twice surrendered his off stump to Rob Henderson in successive balls. As Hendo launched into the high fives, Johnno, his immaculate forward defensive stroke beaten, took off his imaginary helmet and gloves, tucked his bat under his arm and made the most dignified of exits – straight to the lift and back to his room.

Keith Wood

Keith is the world's most aggressive table tennis player and a man from whom I spent most of the tour flinching. His appearance in the massage room would mean either a gentle stroke of the hair or a playful punch in the ribs. He also had a habit of snorting loudly in fellow Lions' ears to make them jump. He reacted to being filmed close up by some fans by taking the video camera and recording a crazy message on it – not quite the memento they had in mind. A very funny guy, he is also a tremendously committed and talented player with huge presence, and is basically hyperactive, especially the day before Tests.

He was all action on the pitch too, cropping up everywhere. A hard hitter with or without the ball, when he tackled someone nearby you could hear the wind being knocked out of them. Not many hookers have a kicking game like his either.

Brian O'Driscoll

Arrogant superstar? Definitely not. He was very approachable and totally immune to the adoring chants of 'Waltzing O'Driscoll' sung by the supporters. Brian's second-half try in Brisbane spoke volumes for his talent. He had the eye to see the gap, the pace to go through it and the footwork to beat the last defender. Stunning. He has everything an attacker could dream of in his box of tricks and his defence is pretty awesome too. His first Test performance was extraordinary and spawned a light-hearted moment in the build-up to the second Test when he turned up at a team meeting in his only clean jersey which just happened to be his Lions shirt. That generated a huge amount of abuse for being big-headed. 'Right, I won't be wearing that shirt again,' he said, embarrassed. He has a very unassuming persona. He's the Monica Seles of table tennis – you've never heard grunting like it.

Jason Robinson

I hold my hand up. I've been a Wigan fan since schooldays but I still had my doubts about whether Jason would make the transition to rugby union without time. He answered all his critics in Australia. Jason had a sensational tour but I don't think we've seen everything from him yet. He is going to be lethal for England. He has no peer as a runner in a one-on-one situation and we have to find more ways of giving him those openings. The more chances he gets, the better he will become – if you can imagine that. Some of the Irish boys weren't too familiar with rugby league and it was a picture to see their faces when they saw his step in training. He reads the game well, too.

He is totally dedicated to his beliefs, his family and his rugby. He listens to Christian music on the way to games and Matt Dawson asked what the music sounds like. 'Well,' said Jason. 'Instead of "Give it to me, baby," like the stuff you listen to, there's a bit more to it.'

Richard Hill

He was a solid, reliable friend and my main sidekick. One of the key players for the Lions until he was whacked out of the tour in the second Test. He played in a different position in the first Test – open-side flanker – than the one he does for England, yet he was outstanding. He is an unsung hero, so Graham Henry may not have known just how good he was before the tour. He will now. Clive Woodward is well aware that Richard is impossible to leave out of any side. His phenomenal work rate simply demands selection. If he had been asked he could have played No. 8 for the Lions as well.

Neil Jenkins

Troubled by a knee injury all tour, Neil was never able to hit the heights of 1997 but he is a great man to have around. Even though we were rivals for the No. 10 jersey, he and Ronan were constantly offering help and advice. If anyone is going to possess an ego, you might expect it to be the world's leading international points scorer, but Jenks is the most modest, understated bloke you could wish to find. People who meet their heroes are sometimes disappointed, but that was not the case for me with Jenks – a Lion and a gentleman.

Jonny Wilkinson's
season – 2000–01

Date	Match	Result		Tournament	Jonny's points
Newcastle					
20/08	v Northampton (h)	27–21	W	Premiership	12
27/08	v Leicester (h)	22–25	L	Premiership	17
02/09	v Sale (a)	27–13	W	Premiership	12
06/09	v Gloucester (h)	18–19	L	Premiership	18
10/09	v Rotherham (h)	34–19	W	Premiership	12
16/09	v Bath (a)	12–19	L	Premiership	12
23/09	v Wasps (h)	59–21	W	Premiership	29
30/09	v Harlequins (a)	20–18	W	Premiership	10
07/10	v Treviso (a)	15–28	L	European Shield	10
15/10	v Cross Keys (h)	99–8	W	European Shield	did not play
22/10	v Begles-Bordeaux (a)	26–18	W	European Shield	16
29/10	v Begles-Bordeaux (h)	39–15	W	European Shield	did not play
04/11	v Rosslyn Park (a)	25–13	W	Tetley's Bitter Cup	did not play
12/11	v Bristol (h)	32–16	W	Tetley's Bitter Cup	22
18/11	v Northampton (a)	18–26	L	Premiership	did not play
26/11	v Saracens (h)	32–27	W	Premiership	did not play
05/12	v London Irish (a)	17–19	L	Premiership	did not play
10/12	v London Irish (a)	33–20	W	Tetley's Bitter Cup QF	23
16/12	v Bristol (a)	14–27	L	Premiership	9
23/12	v Gloucester (a)	13–28	L	Premiership	13
27/12	v Bristol (h)	23–15	W	Premiership	13
06/01	v Sale (h)	37–25	W	Tetley's Bitter Cup SF	22

14/01	v Treviso (h)	30–19	W	European Shield	15
21/01	v Cross Keys (a)	25–11	W	European Shield	did not play
28/01	v Mont-de-Marsan (h)	61–23	W	European Shield QF	17
11/02	v Bath (h)	24–23	W	Premiership	9
24/02	v Harlequins	30–27	W	Tetley's Bitter Cup F	10
06/03	v Harlequins (h)	22–24	L	Premiership	did not play
11/03	v Sale (h)	48–24	W	Premiership	did not play
17/03	v Leicester (a)	7–51	L	Premiership	did not play
28/03	v Wasps (a)	7–44	L	Premiership	did not play
01/04	v London Irish (h)	42–35	W	Premiership	17
10/04	v Rotherham (a)	39–26	W	Premiership	did not play
15/04	v Saracens (a)	29–34	L	Premiership	5
22/04	v Harlequins (a)	12–17	L	European Shield SF	12
28/04	v Bath (a)	9–18	L	Play-off QF	did not play

England

18/11	v Australia (h)	22–19	W	17
25/11	v Argentina (h)	19–0	W	14
02/12	v South Africa (h)	25–17	W	20
03/02	v Wales (a)	44–15	W	10
17/02	v Italy (h)	80–23	W	35
03/03	v Scotland (h)	43–3	W	13
07/04	v France (h)	48–19	W	18

2001 Lions Tour Down Under

08/06	v Western Australia (Perth)	116–10	W	did not play
12/06	v Queensland President's XV (Townsville)	83–6	W	did not play
16/06	v Queensland Reds (Brisbane)	42–8	W	17
19/06	v Australia A (Gosford)	25–28	L	did not play
23/06	v New South Wales Waratahs (Sydney)	41–24	W	19
26/06	v New South Wales Country (Coffs Harbour)	46–3	W	did not play
30/06	v Australia (Brisbane)	29–13	W	9
03/07	v ACT Brumbies (Canberra)	30–28	W	did not play
07/07	v Australia (Melbourne)	14–35	L	9
14/07	v Australia (Sydney)	23–29	L	18

Total appearances 35   **Total points 534**

Index